DOWN TO EARTH

Down to earth

The New Protestant Vision of the Virgin Mary

John de Satgé

A CONSORTIUM BOOK

First American Edition
Consortium Books 1976

ISBN: 0-8434-0607-0
Library of Congress Catalog Card Number: 76-19776

For Margaret
without whose encouragement I should
never have started these studies
R.I.P.

Contents

Acknowledgements

The author wishes to record his thanks for the encouragement given on so many occasions by members of the Ecumenical Society of the Blessed Virgin Mary, and above all by its tireless General Secretary, H. Martin Gillett, K.C.S.G.

Thanks are due to the following for permission to quote from copyright sources:

A. & C. Black Ltd: *The Mother of God*, ed. E. L. Mascall.

Burns & Oates: *The Blessed Virgin*, by Jean Guitton; and *Mary's Place in the Church*, by René Laurentin.

Cambridge University Press: an article by H. A. Williams in *Soundings*, ed. A. R. Vidler.

The Ecumenical Society of the Blessed Virgin Mary: *An Ecumenical Future for Roman Catholic Theology of Mary*, by Donal Flanagan.

The Faith Press Ltd: *Mary, Mother of the Lord and Figure of the Church*, by Max Thurian.

The Fellowship of St Alban and St Sergius: *Orthodoxy and the Conversion of England*, by Derwas J. Chitty.

Hodder & Stoughton Ltd: *After Death*, by J. A. Motyer; *Rome and Reformation*, by J. Atkinson; and *The Unutterable Beauty*, by G. A. Studdert Kennedy.

Inter-Varsity Press: *Modern Art and the Death of a Culture*, by H. R. Rookmaaker.

Thomas Nelson & Sons Ltd: *Atlas of the Early Christian World*, ed. H. H. Rowley.

Penguin Books Ltd: *The Orthodox Church*, by Timothy (now

I

Making the Connections

The notion that Christians who set out to understand their faith and its implications seriously need to understand the Lord's mother and her part is a novel one; that is, except for members of the Roman Catholic Church, the various Eastern Orthodox Churches and some of the more 'catholic' sections of the Anglican Communion. The volume of essays produced in preparation for the Faith and Order conference at Lund in 1952 included a group of studies written to help comprehension between those who took different attitudes towards the Virgin Mary.[1] Individual theologians have written one or two volumes designed to reach across the great divide, but on the whole treatment of the subject until the 1960s has been polemical in tone. 'Catholics do, Protestants do not' has been the underlying theme; and serious studies in the subject have been concerned either to expound or to attack the distinctive doctrines of the Roman Catholic Church. The Fellowship of St Alban and St Sergius is a body which has done great service by its insistence that the problem is not a purely Western one and that there is another major theological tradition with a great deal to say on the subject that is not influenced by the distinctive controversies of Western Christendom.[2]

The situation has changed with startling suddenness. The admission of the Russian Orthodox Church to the World Council of Churches in 1961 marked a turning point. 'Whether we like it or not,' I wrote in a symposium published two years later, 'we are now in a certain relation of explicit Christian fraternity with a large number of people whose devotion to our Lady is an integral part of their faith.' Relations with the Orthodox have increased greatly in the last ten years. But how strangely remote do the words read which I then went on to write: 'On a less official level, Anglicans and Protestants generally are beginning to hold rudimentary dialogue with the Roman Catholic Church.'[3] The founding of the 'Ecumenical Society of the Blessed Virgin Mary'[4] in 1967 and the

I

wealth of important matter, written by Catholic, Protestant, and Orthodox theologians with the avowed intention of critical scrutiny from those of traditions other than the writers' own, which derive from that Society, together with its meetings, central and local, and its international conferences, are but one of many indications that the tempo of ecumenical endeavour has speeded up; and that the particular matter of the Blessed Virgin can no longer be left on one side.

It was, of course, the decision of Pope John XXIII to hold the Second Vatican Council, and his conviction that the *aggiornamento* which he believed God had laid upon the Catholic Church must include serious ecumenism, which led to this startling change. We shall scrutinize many times the Council's teaching on Marian doctrine and its implications; but before a first look at that teaching, we should look both at the historical developments which preceded the calling of the Council and at the separate but related problem of the emotional attitudes which the subject of the Lord's mother arouses. In the paragraphs which follow, I write as a Protestant, expressing as well as I can the reactions with which I am familiar from within my own tradition; I am well aware that there are corresponding and no less well-meant (if misguided) reactions which Protestant attitudes call forth from devout Catholics. The cause of Christian unity has now so far advanced that it is strong enough to withstand the assaults of those from all quarters who are devoted to it expressing in the frankness of love the truth as they see it. Indeed, Christian unity is hampered rather than advanced if it is pursued entirely on the level of theological formulation and through the medium exclusively of the intellect.

Catholics (and Orthodox) do well to take note of the sense of outrage which evangelical Protestants feel at the very existence of a Marian cultus. I use the adjective 'evangelical' deliberately; for much that passes for protestant in modern Christianity lacks the distinctively evangelical emphases which distinguished the original Protestant movement from Martin Luther onwards. Yet 'evangelical' is itself a word full of ambiguity: a source of Protestant shame is the number of evangelical groups who dispute each other's right to that word. As I wrote in the symposium of 1963:

It is notoriously difficult to define an evangelical. As the present

2

writer understands it, evangelicalism is not so much a series of doctrines ... as a set of priorities in interpreting the historic catholic faith. The evangelical is first and foremost a member of the Church and his evangelicalism describes how his membership of the Church is realized. He is a catholic because he shares in the faith of his forebears as it has been handed on in the formularies and worship of the Church; he is an evangelical in his emphasis on the practical authority of the Bible and in his insistence on the need for personal conviction, decision and commitment to accompany sacramental obedience. This priority gives rise to his emphasis on the duty of private Bible-study, on justification through the unmerited grace of God and on the responsible priesthood of the whole People of God; as it does also to his characteristic attitudes towards separated Christians, for he is quick to recognize a community of experience with evangelicals of other denominations.[5]

An evangelical is thus a Christian whose theological convictions are closely related to his personal religion. He has probably reached the settled convictions by which he lives only after struggle of some kind and is consequently deeply attached to them. He (or she; I use the masculine pronoun inclusively) may be a person of the greatest academic distinction, highly sophisticated in all his attitudes; or simple, relatively uneducated, barely able to articulate his faith; or he may stand anywhere between the two. He may belong to any political party or to any religious body that holds the Bible in high regard and holds to the divinity of Christ as the Second Person of the Trinity. But however naïve or however sophisticated, he will hold to one thing as central: the living Christ as the Lord and Saviour through whom he enjoys a personal relationship with God. For the true evangelical this relationship is no cosy affair: though it may at times be expressed in sentimental language, the root of it is anything but sentimental; for it was made possible only through the death of Christ for the putting away of sin. The evangelical is very conscious of the gulf between sinful mankind, in which he shares, and the all-holy God. There is only one bridge across this gulf, the bridge made by the God-man Jesus and his atoning death. The focus of the evangelical's spirituality is therefore Jesus: not the dead Jesus on the Cross—most evangelicals dislike the crucifix—but

3

Jesus who was dead and is alive for ever more, Jesus present through the Holy Spirit to be the believer's Guide and Lord in this world as well as his Saviour for the next.

One immediate consequence of evangelical spirituality is a total intolerance of anything which seems to challenge the unique mediation of Christ, or to suggest that that mediation is not totally adequate. The intolerance must be recognized for what it is: a positive and passionate concern for the glory of God's grace as it has come to humanity in Christ; and a sense of outrage, of disgust even, at the presumption which could suggest that God's provision for human need requires in any way to be supplemented from the human side. It is evident therefore that the evangelical finds it hard even to hear Mary described as mediatrix or co-redemptrix without instantly condemning the phrase as blasphemous. From the same root spring also the characteristic attitudes towards purgatory, prayers for the dead or from them, the Mass viewed as a sacrifice in any sense other than that of the responsive sacrifice of thanksgiving, and above all the necessity of a priesthood to mediate God's forgiveness. Indeed, as one distinguished modern evangelical theologian from whom we shall be quoting extensively, Professor James Atkinson, has put it: 'At the Reformation the real opposite to justification by faith was the belief that forgiveness and acceptance were accorded on the ground of priestly absolution.'[6]

The impression gained thus far may well be that evangelical religion is very subjective in character, constructed out of a religious experience of a certain type. If so, it is due to the inadequacy of the analysis I made earlier in the chapter. The foundation of evangelical religion is the disclosure of God and of the nature of his activities in human life which is contained in the Bible; evangelical religion which does not submit its subjective experience to the judgement of scriptural authenticity is condemned by its own presuppositions. Evangelical theologians (and theologically minded evangelicals—the distinction is worth pondering) insist firmly upon the exclusively normative position of the Bible in establishing what is necessarily to be believed by consistent Christians; and also, by the same criterion negatively applied, what is not to be believed. A considerable difference exists among those who would wish to be known as evangelicals, in the Church of England at least, between those who accept the infallibility of the Bible and those who regard

it as the bearer of the infallible Word rather than that Word en-
scriptured itself.[7] But all evangelicals would unite in commending
the sixth of the Thirty-nine Articles of Religion, with its insistence
that 'Holy Scripture containeth all things necessary to salvation: so
that whatsoever is not read therein, nor may be proved thereby, is
not to be required of any man, that it be believed as an article of the
Faith, or be thought requisite or necessary to salvation.'[8]

That agreement points to the third main doctrinal counterpart
of evangelical spirituality: the belief that the positions maintained
by the 'mainstream' Reformers of the sixteenth century (to be distinguished from the 'left wing' of the Reformation[9]) are those most
consistent with the general tenor of the primitive faith as the
Scriptures show it to have been, and so ought to be taken as normative for the teaching of the Church at all times. Deviations at
any central point from the positions agreed among the Reformers,
and any reformulations achieved by going behind the Reformers to
the witness of the early Church (unless authenticated by appeal to
the Scriptures) are thus highly suspect in evangelical eyes.

Anglican Evangelicals tend to regard themselves as the only
genuine Anglicans, for their historical sense does not allow them to
countenance deviations from the spirit, at least, of the sixteenth-
century Reformers; the catholicizing tendencies of the last hundred
years are seen, where they go behind Reformed positions, as distortions. An interesting by-product of their exclusive claim to
Anglican orthodoxy has been the attitude of some evangelicals
towards the dialogue with Rome which has opened up since the
Second Vatican Council. 'High-Church Anglicans', writes Professor
Atkinson, 'keep up a pretence that Anglicanism is very near to
Rome in its theology and practice. There is not a single Roman
Catholic scholar who would endorse that view, for they are too well
aware of the differences, even the cleavage. They respect an evangelical and understand him; they never can get to grips with the
Anglo-Catholic for they cannot accept his position. Logically he
belongs to Rome and they cannot see why he has not got the sense to
see it. Roman Catholics may be hostile to Protestantism, may not
understand it, but they know that it is a force to be reckoned with
in that as long as it exists it is a condemnation of the catholicism they
profess.'[10]

The evangelical sense of outrage, which is focused most acutely

5

upon the Marian developments in Catholic life and belief, demands to be taken seriously. It will cause dismay to hopes of a quick and easy ecumenism. But where emotional reactions are the outworking of theological convictions about the central Christian doctrines, the dismay may be lightened by rays of hope. For with goodwill on both sides there will be enough common ground to build up that mutual confidence in personal integrity which is needed for considering together the really sensitive issues.

II

There was much in Catholic developments in the century before Vatican II to nourish the Protestant sense of outrage. René Laurentin has a fascinating description of what (after careful justification of the term) he calls 'the Marian movement', in his book *Mary's Place in the Church*.[11] He sees a rebirth of concern for the Lord's mother, which had previously reached a peak in the seventeenth century and gradually declined in the eighteenth, arriving in the 1830s. The new impetus was 'popular' in origin—the series of 'apparitions of our Lady' which began with the Miraculous Medal in 1830 and reached its most famous example with the appearance of the Virgin at Lourdes in 1858. At the other end of the ecclesiastical scale came the definition of the Immaculate Conception by Pope Pius IX in 1854. 'But', writes Father Laurentin, 'this intense spirit of enthusiasm at that time was hampered from within by the theological poverty of the period.'[12] Most of the theological literature supporting the new piety was that of 'up-dated', seventeenth-century authors such as Grignon de Montfort. A few Catholic theologians, notably Newman and Scheeben, were able to contribute in genuine nineteenth-century terms.

Father Laurentin's most interesting point is that the real originator of the distinctive Marian development of the first half and more of the twentieth century, the awareness 'of the fact of Mary's presence in the life of Christians and of the Church', was none other than Cardinal Mercier, the Belgian prelate who, together with the Abbé Portal and the High Anglican layman Lord Halifax, was such a pioneer of catholic ecumenism at the time of the Malines Conversations.[13] Cardinal Mercier put forward his 'idea', which was to have such influence over the next half century and more, in

6

1913: it was for a definition of Mary's mediation.[14] It is curious that a man so concerned with the cause of Christian unity should thus emphasize the one matter above all others which was sure to offend the most deeply held Protestant convictions.

Father Laurentin underlines the tremendous development of the Marian movement in the years between the two World Wars. The theologians, who had been so slow to contribute to the early days of the modern movement, redoubled their efforts. Mariology became a branch of theology in its own right, no longer an appendix to Christology. 'Movements', wrote Father Laurentin of the Marian developments during the pontificate of Pope Pius XII, 'are characterized by their particular orientation. How then can we define the modern Marian movement?'[15] He sees a temporary truce between two potentially rival tendencies in the years before the definition of the Assumption in 1950, and since then, a divergence between the view which starts from Christology and sees the Marian movement as a progressive glorification of Mary according to the analogy of her Son; and, on the other hand, a Mariology which 'situates' (to use a characteristically French theological expression) the place of Mary with that of the Church, the company of her Son's people.

Writing for publication in 1963, Laurentin saw a tension between the 'ecclesiological' current in Mariological studies, born in France and Germany and closely connected with the liturgical movement with its emphasis on the importance of the People of God, clergy and laity together, and with its ecumenical side-implications, on the one hand; and on the other hand, the Marian movement proper, with its tendency to exalt the place of the Lord's mother to a position analogous to that of her Son: a tendency which was itself ultimately a development of the Counter-Reformation in its aspect of Catholic attempts to minimize the slight thought to have been done to the Lord's mother by the Protestant Reformers.

That last point should be carefully noted. We stressed earlier the sense of outrage felt by Protestants at the slight to the all-sufficient atonement of Christ implied by the exaltation of his mother to anything suggesting mediatorial partnership with her Son. We should not ignore the corresponding sense of outrage felt by Catholics at Protestant slurs upon the all-holiness of the woman who was chosen to be the mother of God. 'The stimulus which gave shape' to the

Marian movement as a conscious movement, writes Father Laurentin, 'came from a will to make reparation for the insult done to ... the Virgin Mary by the Reformers.'[16]

The Irish theologian Donal Flanagan corroborates the historical sketch of the Frenchman Father Laurentin in his analysis of the Marian movement; and also in his heartfelt comments on the burden which the spate of Mariological works, often repetitive or of an intolerably narrow specialization, has placed upon the scholar who would keep up to date.[17] Both writers see a healthy change in the drift of Marian development with the change of atmosphere brought about by the pontificate of Pope John XXIII; yet it is interesting to hear Father Laurentin insisting that the Marian fervour of Pope Pius XII, who proclaimed the dogma of the Assumption, 'accompanied a concern for a true sense of proportion, a reticence which astonished some Mariologists, and a moderating influence in which he carried on the ancient tradition of the Holy See in this matter. Pius XII was very guarded about the dogmatization of Mary as mediatrix and co-redemptrix, for he did not wish to do anything which might veil the transcendence of the *unus Mediator*. He systematically avoided the title co-redemptrix in his pontifical acts, and in his directives to the Marian theologians he was careful to warn against exaggeration as well as against understatement.'[18]

It would therefore be wrong to read the statement of the Second Vatican Council concerning the mother of our Lord as in any way a repudiation of the recent Roman Catholic past. It is well known that the statement, contained in the final chapter of the Decree On the Church (*De Ecclesia*, chapter 8), was only agreed after long discussions and, on the part of many of the Council Fathers, with many misgivings; though the narrow majority which passed the revised draft was no doubt increased by the subsequent action of Pope Paul VI in proclaiming Mary to be the Mother of the Church, a title which, however much it may have been implied in the teaching of the Council document, was in fact avoided.[19]

The Vatican Fathers disclaimed any intention 'to decide those questions which the work of theologians has not yet fully clarified',[20] but the very organization of the subject to form part of the treatise on the Church showed that the tradition in Mariology represented, for example, by Father Laurentin was to enjoy not merely toleration but a certain favour in the most authoritative teaching of the Church. Ecumenically that was a great gain, for it brought the subject into relation with theology as understood by all the main traditions of Christendom. Further, the determination of the Council to relate its Mariological assertions to the teaching of the Bible, whether or not that aim was satisfactorily reached, made conversation on the subject of the Virgin possible between Catholic and non-Catholic Christians; for it introduced a shared, biblical, universe of discourse. From now onwards at least, Protestants might talk with Catholics on the subject without the fear that mutual comprehension was only to be achieved with Catholics whose views were suspect to their own authorities.

The specific teaching of the Council will be evaluated in later chapters of this book. For the moment we may summarize it in the words of a distinguished Catholic theologian, Professor Joseph Ratzinger of Tübingen: 'With Mariology now integrated into ecclesiology, the idea of the Church now encompasses the heavenly Church with the result that the eschatological as well as the spiritual aspects of the Church are strengthened. It is now also much clearer that the nature of the Church is not tied up with the temporal dimensions nor fully defined in terms of visible institutions, but that it extends into the future, into an area beyond human intervention and disposition....'[21]

The Mariology of the Second Vatican Council has therefore great ecumenical significance. But it was a conciliatory statement aimed to be acceptable to different schools of thought within the Catholic Church, and it was framed in the knowledge that Protestant friends were by invitation 'listening in' to the discussion. It would therefore be surprising if it had the nature of a definitive statement. The Council Fathers disclaimed such an object: 'It does not', they wrote of the Council, 'intend to give a complete doctrine on Mary, nor does it wish to decide those questions which the work of theologians has not yet fully clarified. Those opinions, therefore, may be lawfully retained that are propounded in Catholic schools concerning her, who occupies a place in the Church which is the highest after Christ and yet very close to us.'[22]

Perhaps the most important development in Catholic thought on the Blessed Virgin to have followed the guidelines indicated by the Council has been for the theology of Mary to 'recognize itself as a

9

doctrine of man and as a doctrine of the work of the Spirit in man'. Dr Flanagan summarizes in those words a main contention in a more recent book by Father Laurentin.[23] Dr Flanagan believes that 'the doctrine of the Holy Spirit, active in the Church, as bond of Christ and the Christian, as *the* Sanctifier, *the* Intercessor', is the only proper context for Catholic reflection on Mary. We shall return to this matter.

III

Protestant response to the Marian emphases of the Council has been mixed. Those of catholic or ecumenical sympathies have found in them a source of encouragement; Mariology, which had seemed to be such a wedge dividing the Roman Catholics even further from other Christians, was now at least subject to acceptable theological controls. Others went further; thus Dr Albert C. Outler thought that 'the identification of the Blessed Virgin as the foremost of all those who have shared in, and who still enrich, the communion of saints may well have the effect, among other things, of recalling Protestants to an important aspect of Christian faith that they have tended to underestimate in their reaction to what was deemed the excesses of conventional Mariology.'[24]

Evangelical protestantism of the type we are mainly concerned with has had little to say on the subject. Dr David F. Wells, who is Associate Professor of Church History and the History of Christian Thought at Trinity Evangelical Divinity School, Deerfield, Illinois, devotes a chapter, or rather an appendix, to what he calls 'Mary: an Unresolved Problem'. His book *Revolution in Rome*[25] deserves careful study, for it shows how deeply a conservative Reformed theologian can enter into the questionings of modern Catholicism without being able to identify himself with them; and how frequently he comes to feel less sympathy for radical alternatives than he does for the traditional positions to which he is opposed. To summarize his position crudely, he sees the Roman system faced with two alternative paths of renewal: reformation according to biblical norms; or the development of a new theology, already to be found among Catholic thinkers, which finds its authority less in the authoritative deposit of revelation, whether in Church dogma or in the Bible, than in the authority of experience.

The latter approach, ecumenically flexible, existentialist, and ultimately subjective (for who decides, and on what criteria, along which directions the authentic Spirit is leading?) is one which a conservative Protestant theologian can as little accept as he can any other 'liberal' form of Christianity. Dr Wells believes that the Second Vatican Council held together with some success the two tendencies, fundamentally opposed as they are; sooner or later, a choice between them must be made. Dr Wells, in fact, is less concerned to respond to his subject than to describe it from outside. We shall consider in a later chapter his estimate of the Council's Mariology.

Professor James Atkinson is an Anglican Evangelical who makes a warmer, though no less vigorous, response to the theology of the Second Vatican Council. It may be that he is able to do so because, as an authority on Martin Luther who has learned much from the subject of his studies, he is able to sit more lightly than Dr Wells to conservative evangelical views of the infallibility of Scripture. 'Recent trends are showing that the Roman Catholic layman is reading his Bible and looks there for the authority of the Word of God as it is evolving in a living Church', he writes. 'This is a sounder view of Scripture than exists in some Protestant circles which look upon the Word as something quarried out of Scripture and tend to fall into the danger of seeing it as an ancient oracle rather than a living Word.'[26]

Professor Atkinson does not deal at any length with the matter of the Blessed Virgin. After describing most vividly the Christ-centredness of Luther's own religion, he explains that it is to that cause that we should look to find the hostility of Luther, as indeed of all his fellow-Reformers, to any worship of the saints or invocation of the Blessed Virgin Mary. Professor Atkinson questions whether the rank and file of the Catholic faithful believe that they are not praying *to* the Virgin or the saints, but *through* them. In other words he shares with the Reformers that sense of outrage which we have earlier considered.[27]

Nevertheless, Professor Atkinson has some most positive suggestions to make for breaking open the deadlock between Rome and the Reformation, and his terms are large enough to provide a context for 'situating' in their proper theological place the Virgin and the saints. Writing as a historian he reviews the course of the

Reformation. He sees that its motivation lay in the discontent which scholarly, responsible theologians and other churchmen felt with the actual state of the Church at the end of the Middle Ages. He recognizes also that the issues were not simply over theology and religion; the movement of reform existed 'within a vortex of social, cultural, and economic revolutions' which marked that time of change.[28] He believes that had the interplay of politics and power allowed the proper theological issues to have been sorted out on their own level, the parties concerned would not have found themselves driven into intransigent positions where agreement was virtually impossible. For there were those at the centre of the Church who were just as urgent for its reform as was Luther. Few of them, however, shared his conviction that the reform must be primarily in the field of theology, and only after that a matter of eliminating scandals and anomalies. There had, however, been moments when history might have taken a very different course. If Leo X, for example, had placed the weight of the papacy behind the cause of reform at the time when Luther's protest was an academic disputation, the Western Church might have been renewed without breaking its unity; in that judgement, Professor Atkinson echoes the Catholic historian Hubert Jedin.[29] The last such moment, according to Professor Atkinson, was at a council held at Regensburg in 1541, when the leader of the Roman delegation was Cardinal Contarini, a man who genuinely understood and was concerned for reform. The meeting failed to reach agreement; Contarini died the next year 'leaving a gap that none could fill. The Italians who had hoped to end division by agreement and compromise now realized that there was very little hope. The conception of a Catholic Reformation disappeared: the idea of a Counter-Reformation took its place.'[30]

The last sentence embodies Professor Atkinson's hopes for the future. At last, with the Second Vatican Council, there are signs that the Roman Catholic Church is prepared to abandon the anti-Protestant outlook which has so coloured its life and thought since the Counter-Reformation, with the result that its own considerable reforms have been carried out in a spirit of countering Protestantism. The positions maintained, by and large, by the Second Vatican Council reflect the views of those few Catholic theologians in recent years who have honestly listened to the Protestants so as to understand them, and, if their criticisms appear valid, to learn from them. The result is what Professor Atkinson calls 'Christendom's second chance'. The new theological climate blown in on the warm wind of Pope John XXIII's encyclical of 29 June 1959 makes possible, not a repeal of the Council of Trent, where the positions of Counter-Reformation were established, but a reappraisal of it.

Professor Atkinson wants the ecumenical debate to return to the possibilities that were open before the Council of Trent, when so many of the best contemporary Roman scholars and leaders hoped to answer Luther and to reform the Church while holding Luther and the evangelicals within the fold. It is not, of course, a matter of ignoring history, or of abjuring it. But the basic issue, however changed the circumstances, is the same as it was at Regensburg: in the Professor's phrase, 'Can Roman Catholicism so reform herself as to take Protestantism into her system?'[31] He thinks the question would best be investigated by a commission of scholars—Protestant and Roman Catholic—meeting over a period of years. Their brief would be to reappraise four matters. The first would be the Reformation; the second, those men and movements who unsuccessfully sought *theological* reformation of Christendom, after Luther's protest but before Trent; the third, the manoeuvrings of Trent and its final decisions; and finally, the whole ecumenical movement today.[32]

Evidently the programme is a long-term one, for its selection of topics is most comprehensive. Parts of it had, in fact, begun before Professor Atkinson wrote, and he gives a list of developments up to that time which were heartening steps in the right direction. The main obstacle, he would seem to say, lies in the Church of England, whose Anglicanism has departed so grievously from the reformed catholicism of the Reformation period. 'Anglicanism', he wrote, 'must set its own house in order and present both to Rome and to the Free Churches a genuine Anglicanism based on a biblical theology; a sound catholic theology; a clear-sighted hold of the formularies, articles, and Prayer Book; and an historical grasp of the last four hundred years—all integrated by sweet reason.'[33] The internal Anglican conversation must result in agreement before Anglicanism can expect to get very far in dialogue with either Rome or the Free Churches.

I have summarized the views of Professor Atkinson at some length because he is one of the few Anglican Evangelical theologians from whom I have found a positive attitude towards the new climate at Rome, expressed in a practical plan of advance. To some extent, events since he wrote those suggestions have overtaken him. In the final section of this book I shall return to his programme, glossing it in the light of the main argument of this book, in a sense of which he might well not approve; but I would add his book to his own list of heartening developments.

IV

We have now indicated sufficiently the context of thought in which this book is situated. Its aim may be simply stated. It is an attempt to find an attitude towards the Lord's mother which will include the essentials of Catholic teaching and at the same time do justice to the central impulses of evangelical Christianity. Professor Atkinson asked as his main question: 'Can Roman Catholicism so reform herself as to take Protestantism into her system?' The first contention of this book is that, in so far as the Vatican teaching represents the position of Rome, it has already done so in that which concerns the Lord's mother. A second point, which follows from the first, is that Protestantism, if it can widen its traditional attitudes so as to include a positive relationship with the Lord's mother, will be thereby greatly enriched. A third point is that this widening of Protestantism will not be achieved simply by adopting Roman Catholic practices but by a return to its own theological sources.

It is for that reason that the title *Mary and the Christian Gospel* has been chosen. I use 'gospel' in the sense in which it has become an accepted term in theological speech in the course of the last forty years: the good news of what God has done through Jesus Christ to end the alienation, estrangement, and hostility that existed between sinful mankind and Himself; the events that centre in Christ, his birth, life, death, resurrection, and ascension, with the release of the Holy Spirit as a new power for the transformation of life; the total provision of God for human need. It is striking to see how far modern scholarship has vindicated the traditional evangelical priorities.

Making the Connections

Protestant polemics have commonly suggested that there is an inherent opposition between the clear acceptance of the gospel on the one hand and a religion which includes personal relationship, the mother of Jesus, and all the saints on the other. Deformations of Christianity in the later Middle Ages had undoubtedly obscured the strong outlines of the gospel, and perhaps it was necessary to cut out altogether the secondary matters if the primary ones were to be seen in the full beauty of their design. But there is no doubt that an impoverishment accompanied the stripping down; much that was of value perished, and some distortion resulted in that which remained. In other words, there is now work of revision to be done on the Protestant side, similar to that which Professor Atkinson so rightly insists must be done by the Catholics. The present work is a small attempt at such Protestant revision in one particular area.

The plan of the book is simple. The next part of the argument, under the title 'Mary and her Son', covers familiar ground from a less familiar angle in order to establish the relation between Christology and Mariology. The third part is concerned with the Lord's mother as her Son's disciple, one among the people whom He has redeemed. The fourth part treats of Mary's special role among her Son's people, as mother. The final section suggests very briefly some of the consequences which follow if the argument is accepted; though the intention there is to leave the matter open for further discussion.

2

Mary and Her Son

I

Jesus of Nazareth continues to haunt the human mind. A secularist of the confident early twentieth century like H. G. Wells could state as a fact that 'in the Gospels all that body of theological assertion which constitutes Christianity finds little support';[1] but he gave most respectful attention to the subject of those assertions. Half a century later revolutionaries of atheist and other ideologies appeal as a matter of course to Jesus as their example; and popular entertainment finds in him and his story an unfailing source of box-office success. A rival religion, Islam, has for over a thousand years accorded him an honourable place in its own traditions.[2]

For some seventeen hundred years something we may loosely call 'mainstream organized Christianity' claimed the monopoly in the interpretation of Jesus, and did so according to just that body of doctrinal assertions which so annoyed H. G. Wells. With the rise of modern methods and techniques in historical investigations, however, scholars, and those who popularized their findings, carried out extensive investigations 'behind the teachings of the Church' and even 'behind the presentation of the written Gospels'. It is no part of the purpose of this book to follow the fascinating course of that prolific and ever expanding field of research.[3] Many of the 'lives' (or other estimates; for only the very unsophisticated could suppose that the materials were present for biography in the normal sense) of Jesus which have appeared in the last century and a half have added greatly to the appreciation of Jesus in the modern world. We may cite a few, often mutually conflicting, often illuminating in some particulars even where their principal thrust may be deemed perverse: E. Renan, *The Life of Jesus*;[4] T. R. Glover, *The Jesus of History*;[5] R. Bultmann, *Jesus and the Word*;[6] G. Bornkamm, *Jesus of Nazareth*;[7] and C. H. Dodd, *The Founder of Christianity*.[8] In this connection the cycle of plays on the life of our Lord by Dorothy L. Sayers, broadcast during the Second

World War under the title of *The Man Born to be King*, should not be forgotten.[9] Perhaps it might be said without ingratitude that subjective factors influencing the assessments of even the most distinguished scholars must not be ignored; though few are so frank and so engaging as Giovanni Guareschi in the first volume of his *Don Camillo* series: 'But if there is anyone who is offended by the conversations of Christ, I cannot help it; for the one who speaks in this story is not Christ, but my Christ—that is, the voice of my conscience.'[10] The Jewish tradition, perhaps not surprisingly, has produced some remarkable assessments of Jesus; notably by Joseph Klausner[11] and, more recently, by Geza Vermes.[12]

Broadly speaking, the reconstructions of the historical Jesus which we have mentioned divide into two groups: those which find justice done to the data in the 'mainstream interpretation', and those which do not.

II

Jesus Christ was an historical figure. That is to say, he was a real human being who lived at a particular time, rubbed shoulders with those other human beings who happened to be alive at the same time and whose paths crossed his; there is a good deal of evidence about the effect he had on those whom he met. At one period of modern scholarship attempts were made to deny his historical existence altogether; he was not an individual, it was maintained, but the mythical personification of certain ideals, fears, and hopes, an object set up for worship in a manner familiar to students of comparative religion. This particular claim is seldom heard today; it was most effectively disposed of by one of the greatest of such students, Sir James Frazer, who wrote *The Golden Bough*. 'The doubts which have been cast on the historical reality of Jesus', he said, 'are in my judgement unworthy of serious attention.'[13]

The reader today who tries to take a fresh look at Jesus, untrammelled by the doctrinal traditions in which his followers have interpreted him, will have some difficulty. The four Gospels, where he will have to go for nearly all his material, show Jesus in a great variety of situations. They are full of local colour, ancient and exotic of course for us, though everyday for the times they treat of. The reader thus has to undertake a measure of historical evaluation before he can be reasonably sure that he is interpreting the material accurately; even so, he will probably remain perplexed by some incidents and some remarks. But a picture will emerge of the central character, a vivid, dramatic, sometimes elusive figure who stands out clearly against his background.

The reader attempting such a task in the 1970s may well find his impressions dominated by that of a man at odds with his environment. Palestine (if we may without prejudice so describe the parts where Jesus lived) was essentially provincial. Its several territories, variously governed on the local level, were all subject to the heavy control of Roman occupation. Age-old ways of obedience to the national God had been modified and tamed in order to survive within that control. The God whom Jesus was brought up to worship was no longer He who had led the remote ancestors through the burning desert, defying the might of Pharaoh's Egypt; who had inspired His armies to rout out the indigenous populations of Canaan; who had through His prophets castigated the kings in Israel and Judah when they forgot their high calling and aped the manners of neighbouring despots, ignoring the stern demands of justice and right dealing. Such a God could not have lived easily in Roman times and the authorities who acted in His name saw to it that obedience was acceptably channelled. The Law was indeed kept, the heroic commemorations duly maintained. The traditions were tailored for survival.

It was all a little tame. There were some who challenged that tameness, our hypothetical reader would discover. A few traces of political challenge, military challenge even, may be discerned in the New Testament itself; but for anything of a systematic account he would have to read in other contemporary sources.[14] It would seem that though Jesus shared the discontent of such challengers with the complacency and compromise of the authorities, he did not wish to head a movement for revolt. There is a paradox here. He spoke often of his 'kingdom' or of 'the kingdom of God' but went out of his way to stress the non-political implication of those terms: 'not of this world'. Indeed there were times when he spoke of obedience to authority as a positive duty.[15] And yet it is not possible to align him with modern advocates of social change brought about through passive protest; on at least one occasion he behaved with unbridled physical violence.[16] He gathered a group of followers far more closely bound to him than the fluctuating crowds who from time to time hung on to the words of a compelling orator, but when those followers tried to defend him at the time of his arrest he stopped them; and he seems to have made little attempt to defend himself in the courts before he went to his shabby execution.

The modern reader would note that Jesus was much concerned with the ills and sadness of ordinary people. He accepted the understanding of these ills and the means of their cure of his time. Thus he was an exorcist in a culture which expected exorcisms, and astonished people only by his unusual success in expelling the evil spirits.[17] He was surprisingly welcoming to certain classes of people commonly regarded (on religious grounds) as outcasts.[18] But on occasions he could be brusque to someone in distress and could speak as if he had no concern for those who did not belong to his own race; and on another occasion, he was immediately helpful.[19] Yet capricious hardly seems a suitable adjective to describe him.

The persons responsible for the Gospels evidently saw his teaching as second only in importance to his actions. Much of the subject matter recorded is in the nature of comment upon the teachings of the Old Testament which Jesus, like all Jews of his day, accepted as the inspired word of God. Yet he was sharply critical of the applications of those writings which the official teachers of the time were making, and indeed on some occasions, at least, of the inspired teachings themselves.[20] His standing as a teacher was perplexing; despite a remarkably precocious appearance as a biblical scholar[21] he does not seem to have belonged to any generally recognized group of teachers.[22] But he enjoyed some sort of *de facto* authority to teach[23] and the best minds among the official teachers were deployed in all seriousness to controvert him; indeed their failure to tie him up in his own words—he managed to turn the tables on them—strengthened their determination to have him suppressed.[24]

The attentive reader would notice a number of incidents, some of them rather weird, where Jesus was evidently drawing the strength he needed to carry out his strenuous and lonely programme.[25] It was impossible to deny that Jesus acted under an intense conviction of divine compulsion; his God was very real to him. There were also a number of occasions when he imparted to his inner ring of followers something of the dynamics he himself lived by.

It could well be reflection upon those dynamics which would lead the reader to consider seriously that element of the miraculous which played so large a part in the gospel narratives. If he seeks help at all from the course of modern biblical study he will find that after every attempt to eliminate the miraculous from the earliest stages of the records about Jesus, scholars have found its total excision impossible; as far back as every technique of historical inquiry can take you, a miraculous element remains as part of the impression which the historical Jesus made upon his contemporaries. The reader will be wise if, at the first stage of his inquiry, he simply registers this as a fact to be taken into account, and avoids any premature assessment of it.

It will perhaps strengthen a feeling he may have gained from other factors that there is that about Jesus which escapes the straightforward investigation he has been making so far.

III

The modern reader will certainly look with great interest at the family circumstances of this puzzling man, Jesus. He will find a fair amount of evidence in the Gospel records, though he may not find it easy to interpret that evidence.

The Gospels according to St Matthew and St Luke both start with long sections describing the origins and birth of Jesus and the particular circles within the complex world of contemporary Jewish life from which he sprang. The sections contain some of the most familiar and well-loved Bible incidents: the visit of the angel at the Annunciation; the birth at Bethlehem, the angels, the shepherds; the wise men from the East, Herod's beastliness, the flight into Egypt, the childhood at Nazareth; and the relations with the cousins Zechariah, Elizabeth, and their son John who was to figure a little ambiguously as the Baptist.[26]

From our modern point of view the most important facts to determine are the effects which the incidents and the relationships would have on the character and the attitudes of the growing child. There were some features which might be supposed to lead to some degree of insecurity: the doubts over paternity, for example; for though Joseph was the legal father and after some preliminary hesitations fulfilled with a good heart his obligations accordingly, there was a tradition reflected in both Gospels (neither St Mark nor St John have anything relevant to say) that though Mary was the mother, her husband was not the real father. But the accounts in both Gospels, much as they differ in detail, both suggest a warm, secure family life which the alarms of Herod's persecution and the life on the move which resulted could have done little to disturb. More difficult, perhaps, would have been the relationships with those who are described in the Gospel narrative as 'the brethren of the Lord': James, Joseph, Simon, and Judas.[27] Were they the younger children of Joseph and Mary? Or the children of Joseph by a former wife? Or the cousins of Jesus, closely associated with Joseph and Mary in a close, 'extended family' unit? We shall see later that there are powerful reasons against the first view, perfectly possible though it is on the evidence of the Scriptures and with a most respectable following in Protestant theology. An attraction of the second view is that it would account, by the familiar mechanisms of sibling jealousy, for the hostility which these 'brethren' showed towards the adult Jesus on at least one occasion.[28] The third view is the one generally favoured by the Roman Catholic Church.

Whatever the precise relationships, the members of Jesus's family played little part in his adult life. His brothers were not numbered among his immediate followers, though one of them, James, played a prominent part in the organization of the church which existed later in his name.[29] On occasions he could draw a contrast between his natural family, bound to him by physicalities, and those followers whose obedience to the will of his 'Heavenly Father' made them into his family in some deeper sense.[30] Yet once again the reader will find the evidence far from clear-cut; for St John's account of Jesus's concern for his mother as she stood by him at his execution suggested a special link and throws interesting light on the enigmatic relation between mother and son in the same writer's account of the wedding feast at Cana.[31] The modern reader will also note with interest that Jesus apparently never married, nor, once his public work had begun, did he have any settled home. He never seems, however, to have lacked for food and shelter (despite a remark contrasting his lot with that of foxes and birds)[32] and there was something about him which made people willing to offer him hospitality ungrudgingly.

The conclusion of such a straightforward reading might well be that Jesus was a man unusually balanced, mature, and in control of his own strange situation. He had presumably profited from a warm family background, emotionally secure however insecure its outward circumstances had been. Great credit must, in modern ways of thought, go to his mother for her protection in his youth and for her subsequent willingness to allow him to go his own way.

It is hard to set down conclusions like that without the suspicion that, however estimable, however sensible they may be, they are rather dull. The fascination which their subject has exercised over the human mind for so long suggests that he himself was anything but dull. Our modern reader, then, may perhaps question the presuppositions with which he approached his task. On the one hand, perhaps the documents he was reading were not designed to yield a modern-style profile of a personality. On the other hand, the subject of the documents may not be wholly understandable in terms of the reader's own experience nor even of the categories between which it is now usual to analyse human character and behaviour. Many of the most reputable studies of Jesus have indeed followed the lines of this chapter; and if they have taken a more sophisticated view of the documents than that of our imaginary reader, they have very often shared his second presupposition. There has been much stress on Jesus as our brother human being; and those ways in which he was different from our highest conceptions of what a man ought to be have been a source of some embarrassment.

An understanding of Jesus which so stresses his 'brotherness' as to play down his 'otherness' may perhaps learn from Frances Cornford's splendid words addressed to 'A Fat Lady Seen from a Train':

> O why do you walk through the fields in gloves,
> Missing so much and so much?[33]

There is indeed so much in the story of Jesus which such an approach cannot but miss; and to that we must now turn.

IV

The stress upon the 'brotherness' of Jesus which has been so marked a feature of Christian theology and apologetics of recent years has been very much needed. Because He has been the central cult figure of a religious tradition extending over so many centuries there has been a tendency to abstract him completely from human life, confining him to the gilded unreality of a separate realm marked 'religious'. The course of Christian theology in its proper task of explicating as fully as human words allow the full dimensions of his being, has stressed his divinity; not indeed necessarily at the expense of his humanity, but in practice it has often seemed so. For the untutored mind (and indeed the tutored) finds it hard to hold together the human and the divine. Church people, anxious to keep their traditions in a time of general uncertainty, have tended to stress the 'otherness' of their Lord; one remembers the outcry from many of the devout during the Second World War which greeted the broadcast of Dorothy L. Sayers's magnificently orthodox cycle of plays on the life of Jesus; she made him speak in ordinary language.[34] There has thus very properly been in our day a revival of emphasis upon the real humanity of Jesus. Unfortunately, however, that emphasis has sometimes gone so far as to eliminate the other elements in the Christian faith concerning Jesus. There has been talk not merely of his humanity, but of his humanity 'without remainder'. It is the tendency to eliminate those aspects of Jesus which are alien to common human experience which makes an account of him such as our imaginary reader gave earlier in this chapter so untrue to its subject and so dull.

The climate of the opinion is important. The writer of Christian theology has a heavy responsibility to express what he believes to be the truth in terms which will not put unnecessary difficulties in the way of his readers. And most people today find those elements in the biblical picture of Jesus which lie outside the boundaries of normal human experience to be very hard to take. And perhaps perversely, the minority who live within the orthodox Christian tradition find the same elements to be a wall of defence against the cold rationalities of modern secularism. Such factors have combined to make many Catholic as well as Protestant exponents of the faith emphasize the humanity of Jesus. So it is in that direction that we find the Dominican theologian Father Jelly pointing the main thrust of his paper *The Place of the Blessed Virgin in a Secular Age*, one of the most useful contributions to our subject to have appeared recently. 'The reality of Christ's humanity as revealed in the redemptive Incarnation must be emphasized.'[35]

Father Jelly writes as a Catholic concerned to equip his fellow Catholics better in the commending of their faith to the modern world. An essential preliminary is to free them from a 'religiosity' which 'denies any inherent value to the secular order of creation and sees some form of sacralization as the only way to save and sanctify the secular'. Of course, Father Jelly is far too good a theologian not to be aware of the opposite error : so to overstress the place of the secular in the divine purpose that no room is left for anything else; or, in terms of understanding Jesus, to emphasize his humanity so heavily that there is 'no remainder' and that to speak of his 'divinity' is merely to point to the totally satisfactory fulfilment of his manhood.

No one could quarrel with Father Jelly's insistence on the reality of Christ's manhood. His fear of 'religiosity' no doubt reflects a tendency in current catholicism. But in writing from a Protestant background I would wish to stress far more than he does the opposite danger. I do not find among my co-religionists an alarming amount of religiosity. I find instead a reduction of Christian obedience to ethicism: an ethic of behaviour, a code of conduct. Sometimes (among the more conservative) it is an ethic centring on personal, family, or sexual morality; sometimes (among the more progressive) it centres upon social affairs. In either case the danger is that a concern for the right ordering of things in this world will exclude any concern with what lies beyond it. Many protestants would endorse Matthew Arnold's definition of religion as 'morality tinged with emotion'. The ethics of Jesus, his teaching, the Sermon on the Mount, following an example—those are some of the phrases that spring most naturally to the protestant (which includes the Anglican) mind. If the characteristic catholic error of religiosity is related to a view of Jesus which surrounds him with so much divinity as to deny his humanity and consequently to undervalue the whole sphere of the human, the protestant error of ethicism connects with a view of him as just another man; a better man no doubt, the perfect one perhaps. Jesus is one of a series, the religious teachers. Moses, Buddha, and Confucius are his brothers. He is one of us 'without remainder', a reminder of what we might be. What has dropped out is a proper element of discontinuity.

It will be convenient at this early stage in our argument to avoid the technical terms of Christology (as that branch of theology which treats of the understanding of Jesus is called) and speak simply of the 'brotherness' of Jesus, and his 'otherness'. By 'brotherness' is meant those aspects which chime readily with our own experience as it is or as we can imagine it might be. By 'otherness' are signified those features in the New Testament picture of Jesus which we instinctively feel to be 'different'. This is a loose classification at at least two levels. First, it lets in a great deal of subjectivism: what is 'different' to one man may seem 'brotherly' to another. And more theologically, the proposed classification does not commit us to the undesirable assignment of the 'brotherly' bits to his humanity and the 'otherly' bits to his divinity. A cardinal insistence of classical theology is that the humanity of Jesus was just as human as our humanity, but that it was humanity unvitiated by the infections of sin. It is precisely at this point—the possibility of a wholly righteous anger is an obvious example—that the proper element of discontinuity between his human nature and ours referred to in the previous paragraph is so important.

The Gospel writers, as our observant reader will have seen, leave no doubt that there was a side to Jesus which his contemporaries found most uncomfortable. It is indeed remarkable how many incidents are recorded where those who met him did not at all enjoy the encounter. Nor was the disquiet which he brought confined to any one set of people: strangers, friends, Pharisees, disciples, and ordinary people in synagogue or countryside were sometimes ill at ease. Even those who were closest to him were very much aware of the difference between him and themselves; there was none of the easy familiarity as between equals. A brief summary of two groups of incidents from the Gospel narratives will serve to show between them the main ways in which he was 'different'.

The first is that of Jesus striding out ahead of his disciples. St Mark records the classical example.[36] 'And they were on the road, going up to Jerusalem, and Jesus was walking ahead of them; and they were amazed and those who followed were afraid.' An interesting exercise is to set side by side the instances of people being 'amazed' at Jesus. The verbs used in the original Greek tend to be ones of strong meaning; consternation was in the air. In the case just cited the verb carries the sense of awe. St Mark had used it on an earlier occasion.[37] Jesus, teaching in the Capernaum synagogue, had successfully exorcized a man possessed by an evil spirit. 'And they were all amazed,' we read of those who were present, 'so that they questioned among themselves, saying, "What is this? A new teaching! With authority he commands even the unclean spirits and they obey him."' A similar atmosphere colours St Mark's account of the storm on the lake which Jesus stilled.[38] The disciples in the boat were 'filled with awe and said, "Who then is this that even the wind and the sea obey him?"' St Mark's unfolding of the story goes on immediately to the episode on the other side of the lake where Jesus expelled an evil spirit which promptly stampeded a herd of swine to their death. The news got around and people came out to investigate. They were told about the two things, the healed man and the drowned pigs; 'and', we read, 'they began to beg Jesus to depart from their neighbourhood.'[39]

The 'otherness' of Jesus striding out ahead of the disciples, causing consternation to them as much as to people who had no intimate links with him, is too deeply imbedded in the Gospel narrative to be written out of it; it was the otherness experienced by those who rubbed shoulders with him and yet found him to be different. The second group of incidents which illustrate this theme belongs to the period of the early Church, when Jesus was no longer there to be rubbed shoulders with, yet somehow he was still there. I do not mean the strange happenings of that interval which the first three Gospel writers (but not the fourth) describe between the Resurrection and the Ascension; but the experience of the Church in the years which followed.

A good example comes at the end of St Mark's Gospel. 'So then the Lord Jesus, after he had spoken to them, was taken up into heaven and sat down at the right hand of God. And they went forth and preached everywhere, while the Lord worked with them and confirmed the message by the signs that attended it.'[40] The ending of St Mark's Gospel is notorious for the critical problems it presents. The best manuscripts do not include the passage where those words occur, and there is an alternative ending; but many scholars think that either the original ending is lost, or else that the book ended arbitrarily but with dramatic force at verse 7. The very uncertainty of the text bears witness to the fact that we are dealing with a continuing experience in the early Church. The final words attributed to Jesus according to St Matthew make the same point of his continued presence in the continuing work of his followers: 'Go, therefore, and make disciples of the nations', he commands; and ends with the promise, 'Lo, I am with you always, to the close of the age.'[41]

The examples given so far point to the belief of the early Christians that Jesus their Lord was still present with them, even after his departure, as they worked for the extension of his 'kingdom'. St Matthew's Gospel, from which it is possible to read off so much of the corporate life of the local church in which it was compiled, demonstrates a similar conviction that Jesus's presence might be counted on in the settlement of internal disputes. 'If your brother sins against you,' Jesus is reported as saying to his disciples, 'go and tell him his fault, between you and him alone. If he listens to you, you have gained your brother. But if he does not listen, take one or two others along with you, that every word may be confirmed by the evidence of two or three witnesses.' If the man is still obstinate, he is to be taken before the whole assembly of the faithful; and if he still persists, the assembly must exercise its power of binding and loosing by treating him as outcast from the community for the duration of his contumaciousness. The local church may dare to do this, Jesus concludes, because 'where two or three are gathered together in my name, there am I in the midst.'[42] Echoes of this belief may be heard in some of the sections of St Paul's letters where he is dealing with pastoral problems.[43]

But it is to St Luke, in the Acts of the Apostles, that we should go for the most striking example of the otherness of Jesus, absent yet present. The wretched Saul, authorized by the Sanhedrin to stamp out dangerous talk about Jesus which had spread to Damascus, was struck down on his journey by a blinding light. He heard a voice saying to him, 'Saul, Saul, why are you persecuting me?' He said, 'Who are you, Lord?' and got the reply: 'I am Jesus whom you are persecuting.' Jesus, the executed blasphemer himself! Saul had supposed himself to be after the followers of a man whom public execution had well and truly put paid to.[44]

V

Jesus striding ahead; Jesus absent yet present. The two pictures may stand for the otherness of Jesus who is also our brother. The reconstruction of Jesus as an ordinary (if superb) human being attempted by our imaginary reader of the Gospels earlier in this chapter, is thus doomed to failure. For Jesus the man is also a mystery; a mystery in the sense that Rudolf Otto gave the word in his great book *The Idea of the Holy*:[45] *mysterium tremendum et fascinans*, the mystery which causes fear and which yet attracts. Recent theological writing, especially where it has been directed towards the unbeliever, has emphasized too much the *fascinans* element, the winsomeness. The result has been to distort the evidence which can be recovered from the experience of those who had known him in the days of his earthly life and in the first years which followed. The mystery of Jesus is that he is both brother and other.

Which means that his mother was the mother of one who was both brother and other; and it is to her that we now turn to see what light the study of her may throw upon the mystery that is her Son. There are two main ways of carrying forward such study: the descriptive, where the materials to be used are the several incidents where she figures in the New Testament; and the dogmatic, where the raw material is the tradition of teaching about her which the Church, in its long process of trying out possible ways of speaking, has found to be least inadequate.

The series of word-pictures in the early chapters of St Luke and St Matthew have a haunting beauty which makes it distasteful to analyse them. Yet scholars agree that these pictures were from the first not meant to be taken simply at their face value; whatever their origins, they were worked into the Gospels in order to say from the start something important about the one who is the main subject of the Gospels. In other words they are not simple, artless tales, nor are they simple chronicles; but they are tales and chronicles which have been made the vehicles of important doctrine. We should therefore not be afraid to draw large conclusions from small details. We said that the first method of approaching the Lord's mother was the descriptive; that word must be understood in a sense large enough to include the meanings which the words selected to make the descriptions suggest are there.[46]

It is St Luke who has the most to say about Mary and we must read his presentation of her with detailed care. But St Matthew's bold statement that Mary was found to be with child by the Holy Spirit[47] makes the same point as St Luke with his account of the Annunciation, and the message of the angel: 'The Holy Spirit shall come upon you and the power of the Most High shall over-shadow you; therefore the child to be born will be called Holy, the Son of God.'[48] What could express more strikingly than those two phrases the whole mystery of Jesus in his otherness from us and his brotherness to us?

Our inquiry into Mary, mother of her Son, has now reached a new stage. We have considered her in modern terms as the mother simply of a man; we have noted the ways in which her Son was 'different'; and with a closer study of St Luke's presentation we shall see her as the mother who bore the one who fulfilled her people Israel's historic hopes. A great deal of technical study has been devoted in recent years to St Luke as a writer. The emphasis, so general in the first half of this century, upon his concern with historical accuracy rather than theological interpretation, has been greatly modified and he is now seen to be as much a theologian as an historian; and a convenient theological key for opening his distinctive thought is that Jesus for all his strangeness was and remains Israel's true king. It is this conviction which controls the selection and arrangement of the material used to describe the circumstances of that king's birth, and also of the part played by his mother.

The king in question was to be the king hoped for in the expecta-tion of Jewish traditions; the Messiah ('anointed one' in English, *Christos* in Greek), the deliverer-king descended from the great King David. There was a certain amount in the Old Testament, and a considerable amount more in the Jewish writings coming from the period after the Old Testament proper had been completed, which gave vivid pictures to shape the messianic hopes of pious Jews. One of the most important of these was that the Messiah would be preceded by a prophet in the old, heroic style, a prophet

who was to be a new Elijah. St Luke therefore begins his narrative
with the birth of this forerunner who will call the people to repentance so that they may recognize their king. Zechariah the Temple
priest and his wife Elizabeth do not merely give birth to the forerunner John; that birth is described in terms of prophecy. The
spirit of Elijah will be upon the child, but as the familiar story
unfolds, we see that the Spirit is already present in the words of
the angel and in the mother herself as she greets her cousin who
is carrying the child her own child is to prepare the way for.
Zechariah himself, struck dumb by the angel's words, has his own
tongue loosed when he orders his son to be named John; he is
then filled with the Holy Spirit to prophesy, 'Blessed be the Lord
God of Israel.'

The combination of circumstances here described makes it clear
that a new age is beginning: the new age of the outpouring of
prophecy (dormant so long in the last two or three dreary centuries
of Hebrew history) which the earlier prophets had said would mark
the time of the Messiah's coming. The events St Luke intends to
describe are no mere continuation of contemporary Jewish religion.
That had grown hard, as if it were arthritic, and its shell will have
to be broken; but it will be broken in such a way as to show a
continuity underlying the discontinuity. The new thing about to
happen is the true and legitimate development of what has gone
before; there were good legal as well as theological reasons for
St Luke to insist on that point.[49] The *status quo* in Jewish religion
will therefore be broken from within, by a fresh upsurge of the
same energies which had earlier produced it but which latterly had
been sadly drained and shamefully tamed.[50] St Luke tells us by
the manner as well as the matter of his first two chapters that the
events he has to describe are 'according to the Scriptures'.

In the sixth month the angel Gabriel was sent from God to a
city of Galilee named Nazareth, to a virgin betrothed to a man
whose name was Joseph, of the house of David; and the virgin's
name was Mary. And he came to her and said, 'Hail, O favoured
one, the Lord is with you!' But she was greatly troubled at the
saying, and considered in her mind what sort of greeting this
might be. And the angel said to her, 'Do not be afraid, Mary,
for you have found favour with God. And behold, you will

conceive in your womb, and bear a son, and you will call his
name Jesus.

He will be great, and he will be called the son of the Most High;
And the Lord God will give him the throne of his father David.
And he will reign over the house of Jacob for ever
And of his kingdom there will be no end.'[51]

There could hardly be a more striking introduction to the theme
of the messianic kingdom. 'Great David's greater Son' is to be
born. The ancient theme of David's kingdom is taken over and
developed or transformed into something greater than had been
known even in the most distinguished periods of the Hebrew
monarchy. The messianic kingdom which, one gathers, had been
the inspiration, or the dream, or the escapism in the depression
centuries of Persian, Greek, and Roman times was at last to be
given substance. The gnarled old root was to produce a new shoot
of endless vitality. And all this was to begin in the darkness of
Mary's womb. Small wonder that she was troubled. St Luke grasps
firmly one of the most forbidding of apologetic nettles; the absurd
contrast between the magnitude of the Christian claims and the
insignificance of the individuals through whom they were advanced.
But the kingdom he was concerned with was no ordinary one.
It was authentic all right; was it not attested by prophecy and for
good measure by the greatest of the angels, Gabriel, who stands
in the presence of God?[52] But this kingdom was to come by the
strange entrance of frail humanity.

And Mary said to the angel, 'How can this be, since I have
no husband?' And the angel answered her: 'The Holy Spirit shall
come upon you, and the power of the Most High shall overshadow
you. Therefore the child to be born of you will be called Holy,
the Son of God.'[53] Mary has expressed her sense of inadequacy
for the destiny opening so awesomely before her: become mother
of the more-than-davidic king? Mary's question, however it be
interpreted,[54] is concerned with the physical. The angel's answer
is not made directly to the question she has asked; it would stand
whatever her matrimonial state. For the angel insists that the
one to be born will not derive simply from the process of human
generation. Whether or not it is caused by natural means does not
alter the fact that God's intervention gives it a quite unusual

importance. The womb is Mary's but the power which casts its mysterious influence there is the power of the Most High. Mary has no need to worry about her inadequacy for the task. As it was not of her choosing, so it will not be her excellence that fulfils it. It is because of the Spirit's working that the child to be born will be what it will be.

St Luke has now introduced the second of his great themes. The events he is setting down in order are not merely the fulfilment of prophecy; they are the direct result of God's activity through the Spirit. They do not depend upon the stronger human qualities; indeed, the channels through which they happen will be most conspicuously those of human weakness. The angel emphasized this point as he went on to speak of Mary's kinswoman Elizabeth who though well past the age of childbearing had produced a son. 'For with God', the angel concluded magnificently, 'all things are possible.'[55] The words clearly echo the Genesis passage[56] where Sarah's bitter laughter at the prospect of a son was silenced. It is scarcely possible to avoid the theological term 'grace' to describe what is happening; and it is certainly proper at this point to remember that the angel's introductory greeting to Mary, 'Hail, O favoured one', was expressed by the verbal form of the Greek word for grace. The kingdom to be established among men was to be a kingdom of grace, the work of God bringing into actuality that which he had earlier, through the prophets, promised.

'Behold, I am the handmaid of the Lord; let it be to me according to your word.' With Mary's answer, a third main theme joins the other two. The kingdom brought into being by the power of God's Spirit demands acceptance or rejection by those to whom it is presented. It is most important to grasp the order of these themes and their interrelationships; response to God's word is—response. It is reaction, not initiative; the answer to grace, not the cause of its release. With Mary's response, the first narrative she figures in is complete. The angel departed from her. St Luke could hardly have said more effectively that the action has now begun, its essential constituents dramatically introduced.

There follows the meeting between the two pregnant women. Mary goes to see her elderly kinswoman who, filled again with the testifying Spirit, blesses her; the terms of the blessing will be considered later. Mary then breaks into the prophetic song which is called the Magnificat. Heard in the context St Luke has already provided, the song brings together the three themes. It is essentially an amplification of Mary's 'Let it be to me according to your word.' Her soul magnifies the Lord because of the great things He has done. Commentators have caught echoes from many a triumphant shout of Old Testament times, and of them most persistently from Hannah's song.[57] The theme of grace rings clear as a bell in Mary's song; the Lord whom she magnifies has done it all. The theme of prophecy fulfilled is implicit in all the Old Testament echoes with their allusions to God's care for his people in the past; and it is made explicit at the end: 'He has helped his servant Israel in remembrance of his mercy, as he spoke to our fathers, to Abraham and his posterity for ever.' With the Magnificat, the third basic theme of response to the first two themes has been completely stated, and St Luke rounds off the incident with one of those summarizing statements which are such a feature of his editorial work: 'And Mary remained with her about three months, and returned to her home.'

St Luke then describes what happened after the birth of Zechariah and Elizabeth's son John, reaching a climax with Zechariah's inspired song which we know as the Benedictus; and a summary statement of John's excellent growth ends chapter 1. Chapter 2, of course, begins with the exquisite story of Christmas. Mary is hardly mentioned except for the centrally important activity of giving birth to her Son. The shepherds on the nearby hills were visited by angels and in their turn visited the manger at Bethlehem. 'And when they saw it, they made known the saying which had been told them concerning the child', we read. 'And all who heard it wondered at what the shepherds told them. But Mary kept all these things, pondering them in her heart.'[58]

Two further incidents round off the cycle of events which St Luke associates with the birth of Jesus. The first was his circumcision, when he was named in accordance with what the angel of the Annunciation had declared ('You shall call his name Jesus, for he will save his people from their sins,' the angel who had appeared in a dream to Joseph had said, in St Matthew's equivalent).[59] The second episode must be dealt with at greater length.

It is what the Anglican Book of Common Prayer calls 'The

Presentation of Christ in the Temple, commonly called the Purification of St Mary the Virgin'. (The question of whether St Luke has run together two separate ceremonies[60] is not important for the present discussion.) Joseph and Mary brought Jesus to the Temple for the appropriate ritual purposes. They were met there by an aged man called Simeon, one whose spirit was sensitive to the ways in which the Holy Spirit was acting in the affairs of Jesus. This person took the young child in his arms and blessed God over him in the words we know as Nunc Dimittis. 'And', we read, 'his father and his mother marvelled at what was said about him.' Simeon then blessed the parents and addressed some most significant words to the mother: 'Behold, this child is set for the fall and the rising of many in Israel, and for a sign that is spoken against (and a sword will pierce through your own soul also), that thoughts out of many hearts may be revealed.'[61] A prophetess called Anna, evidently one of the same devout circle, added her own word of testimony.[62]

The sword of which Simeon spoke began to pierce Mary's heart in the incident which ends St Luke's account of the birth and infancy of Jesus. Jesus was a boy of twelve and so coming up to the time of his Bar Mitzvah, where he became a member of the Jewish commonwealth in his own right. The family had been up to Jerusalem on pilgrimage with a crowd of other Nazareth people. His parents suddenly discovered that Jesus was nowhere to be found in the returning party. They went back to Jerusalem; and after what must have been three agonizing days they found him in the Temple, showing astonishing perspicacity as he took part in learned discussions there. And his mother said to him, 'Son, why have you treated us so? Behold, your father and I have been looking for you anxiously.' And he said to them, 'How is it that you sought me? Did you not know that I must be in my Father's house?' And they did not understand that saying which he spoke to them. And he went down with them, and came to Nazareth, and was obedient to them; and his mother kept all these things in her heart.'[63]

A mother's primary function is to give birth to her child. But motherhood does not end with parturition. She has to protect and feed her child; and to know when the time has come to let him go his own way. The alterations and adjustments in the relationship between mother and child are hard enough to cope with in the ordinary run of things; perhaps we, with our acute experience of the 'generation gap', can appreciate the problems of Mary and Jesus with greater clarity than our forebears. But in that unique case where the child had been born through the power of the Most High to occupy the throne of his father David in a kingdom that should have no end, the problems of adaptation are beyond imagination. The summary statement with which St Luke ends this major division of his Gospel suggests that they were satisfactorily solved: 'And Jesus increased in wisdom and in stature and in favour with God and man.'[64]

VI

The narratives just examined lay down the main lines of the relationship between Jesus and his mother throughout his life, as St Luke would have us understand it. There are, however, one or two other episodes in his Gospel which throw light on the matter, not so much by introducing new elements as by showing how the relationships already stated in terms of infancy were managed during adult life. There are two passages in particular which demand our attention, and at first sight neither of them is particularly flattering to either party.

Then his mother and his brothers came to him, but they could not reach him for the crowd. And he was told, 'Your mother and your brothers are standing outside, desiring to see you.' But he said to them, 'My mother and my brothers are those who hear the word of God and do it.'[65]

The circumstances of the other passage are very different, but the general tone is much the same. 'And as he said this, a woman in the crowd raised her voice and said to him, "Blessed is the womb that bore you and the breasts that you sucked." But he said, "Blessed rather are those who hear the word of God and keep it." '[66]

The first of these passages is interesting because it is to be found in St Mark's Gospel as well. The version of it in St Mark reads far more plainly as a rebuke to Mary than does St Luke's way of putting it. St Mark[67] makes it the climax of the opposition which Jesus had begun to find in the early part of his public work. The suggestion had been made that his success in expelling demons was the result of a pact he had made with the powers of evil. His reply had been the well-known remark about blasphemy against the Holy Spirit. A crisis had been reached; and Mark's suggestion seems to be that the family of Jesus intervened in an attempt to control the excesses of their fanatical kinsman. In this context there is no doubt what Jesus means; his true family is not his own flesh and blood, but those who do the will of God.

The force of these words in St Luke (St Matthew has them in a similar context to St Luke) is rather different. The background situation there is one not of controversy but of teaching in the presence of a well-disposed crowd. He has been teaching in particular about the Kingdom, whose characteristics are communicated in a series of parables centring round that of the sower, the seed, and the soil. His mother and his brothers approached him, he was told; and his remark about them reads as an example defining the relationships of the Kingdom he has been speaking about. These relationships, even now starting to come into being, are established by obedience to God's Word perceived and obeyed. Relationships shared between citizens of the Kingdom are deeper than merely physical ones. It was indeed possible for natural ties to prevent discipleship and so to frustrate a share in the Kingdom. There was a moment of dangerous popularity when Jesus put it in an extreme form: 'If anyone comes to me and does not hate his own father and mother and wife and children and brothers and sisters, yes, and his own life, he cannot be my disciple.'[68] For St Luke, it is the cost of discipleship which impels Jesus to indicate his true family, not, as in St Mark, a situation of conflict.

There are indeed good grounds to suppose that St Luke included the physical family of Jesus, or at least his mother, within the deeper relations constituted by the discipleship of the Kingdom. 'My mother and my brothers are those who hear the word of God and do it'—those words are almost an echo of certain things St Luke had earlier written of Mary. There was her act of acceptance, 'Let it be to me according to your word'; her reaction to the shepherds at the manger, when she 'kept all these things, pondering them in her heart'; and perhaps most strikingly, the conclusion of that disturbing and testing affair with her twelve-year-old Son, when his mother 'kept all these things in her heart'.

The impression that St Luke means us to understand that the

Lord's mother is included in the new family of the Kingdom gains strength from setting the passages just discussed alongside the exchange with the woman in the crowd: 'Blessed is the womb which bore you and the breasts that you sucked'—'Blessed rather are those who hear the word of God and keep it.' There is a great likeness between those two words and a passage from the birth narratives which we have not hitherto considered. Elizabeth, filled with the Holy Spirit, blessed her visiting cousin: 'Blessed are you among women, and blessed is the fruit of your womb! ... And blessed is she who believed that there would be a fulfilment of what was spoken to her from the Lord.'[69]

Mary's blessedness is a theme of capital importance, and in elucidating it we shall return on several occasions to the present text. For the moment it is only necessary to underline St Luke's obvious point. Mary's blessedness lay in believing the Word of the Lord and in doing what that Word implied. We should therefore understand the apparent rebuffs or rejection in the light (for St Luke's presentation, at least) of that controlling belief. It is no surprise to find that when, at the start of his second volume, St Luke names those who were in the upper room at Jerusalem waiting and praying for God's further action, Mary the mother of Jesus figures on the list; so, perhaps more surprisingly, do his brothers.[70]

VII

The familiar words of the so-called Apostles' Creed,[71] 'conceived by the Holy Ghost, born of the Virgin Mary', convey in their own dogmatic manner the disjunction as well as the similarity which our survey of the Gospel pictures made so clear between Jesus and ourselves. The function of dogmatic theology is to clarify the basic evidence of Christian faith, relating together as justly as may be the several parts of the faith and establishing their true proportions.

The phrase 'conceived by the Holy Ghost' is more than a paraphrase of the 'Annunciation' passages in St Matthew and St Luke. It shows those passages are not merely marginal to the Christian faith, as an attempt to reconstruct it solely on the basis of the Gospels might suggest. The phrase in its context sets the whole story of Jesus fair and square in the counsels, the activity, and the being of God. In doing so it is indeed not going beyond the New Testament, except in its precision. The nature of our previous survey confined its attention to the Gospels, for our concern was with the life of Jesus. We did not look at the Epistles, for they were letters written to people who were not living as Christians sustained by the memory of Jesus so much as by the power of God which they found through their experience of Him as the one who had risen from the dead and who now connected them with the very source of life itself. The Epistles were written to remind local groups of Christians of the faith they already knew, but whose implications they were at some points contradicting, ignoring, or neglecting. The Epistles do not therefore provide any primary, systematic teaching of the faith. They allude to it, writing as between those who had the basic subject-matter in common. Reading the Epistles is like reading one side of any correspondence between members of a family. Fortunately most of the writers repeated a good many of the matters they wished to comment on, or at least gave summaries; fortunately, too, Christian readers today belong to the same family, and our fundamental traditions have not changed beyond recognition with the centuries. Finally, in approaching the Epistles, we should realize that while their manner and sometimes their matter sounds so different from that of the Gospels, they were nearly all written at a time closer to the events the Gospels describe than were the Gospels themselves in their final form.

The Epistles describe Jesus time and again with resounding phrases which point to the most intimate connection with God. It is not merely St Paul, as people have said, who wished to minimize the divinity of Jesus, claiming that St Paul had distorted the simple faith of the Gospels. The opening sections in particular of any of the Epistles will reveal in one idiom or another claims about Jesus which accord him a greater than human standing; and in any case more modern scholarship inclines to the view that some of the most striking passages are quotations from very early Christian hymns which St Paul is adopting for teaching purposes. If the contentions of these scholars are right and the 'big' statements about Jesus come from hymns rather than from the logic of theological reflection, it is a further indication of how inevitable it was for those who had given their allegiance to Jesus to worship him; that is, to behave towards him in a way that is only proper towards

God. Passages like the following form a bridge between the language of the Bible and that of the Church:

Have this mind among yourselves, which is yours in Christ Jesus, who, though he was in the form of God, did not count equality with God a thing to be grasped, but emptied himself, taking the form of a servant, being born in the likeness of men. And being found in human form he humbled himself and became obedient unto death, even death on a cross. Therefore God has highly exalted him and bestowed on him the name which is above every name, that at the name of Jesus every knee should bow, in heaven and on earth and under the earth, and every tongue confess that Jesus is Lord, to the glory of God the Father.[72]

He is the image of the invisible God, the firstborn of all creation; for in him all things were created, in heaven and on earth, visible and invisible ... all things were created through him and for him.... For in him all the fullness of God was pleased to dwell, and through him to reconcile to himself all things ... making peace by the blood of his cross.[73]

... In these last days he has spoken to us by a Son, whom he appointed heir of all things, through whom also he created the world. He reflects the glory of God and bears the very stamp of his nature, upholding the universe by his word of power. When he had made purification for sins, he sat down on the right hand of the Majesty on high, having become as much superior to the angels as the name he has obtained is more excellent than theirs.[74]

Church people will be familiar with the preceding quotation from its place in the liturgical Epistle for Christmas Day. The example which rounds off this brief selection from the many New Testament celebrations of Jesus as Lord comes from the Christmas Gospel:

In the beginning was the Word, and the Word was with God, and the Word was God. He was in the beginning with God; all things were made through him and without him was not anything made that was made.... And the word became flesh

39

and dwelt among us, full of grace and truth; we have beheld his glory, glory as of the only Son from the Father.[75]

VIII

The conviction that Jesus could only properly be treated as God raised many difficulties for serious people in the ancient world, and it does so, too, in the world of today. Then, as now, attempts have been made to soften the belief in such ways as to accommodate it better to prevalent categories of thought. The enterprise of commending the Christian faith has always been a delicate one. It is so easy from the best possible motives to make some modification which, while easing an immediate problem, causes serious damage to the integrity of the faith as a whole, damage which may not be perceived for some time. Another difficulty comes from the way a word may change its meaning from one cultural setting to another, so that merely to repeat an ancient phrase may well give a different meaning from that which it originally carried. There is the related difficulty of translating from one language to another, where equivalent words may move out into different associations of meaning.

An immediate problem was that the actions which the first missionaries (as well as all missionaries of the Christian faith since) proclaimed to have been God's work through Jesus, his life, death, and resurrection, had all happened in the Jewish tradition. 'In accordance with the Scriptures' rings as a watchword through the apostolic preaching. The Scriptures were the Old Testament. They were written in Hebrew, no longer a currently spoken language at all, though one preserved for religious purposes; Palestinian Jews spoke the related language, Aramaic. For a couple of hundred years there had been colonies of Jews permanently resident in most of the important urban centres of the Mediterranean world, and for their benefit an authorized translation of the Scriptures had been made into Greek, which was the most generally spoken language of the period. Jesus himself almost certainly spoke and taught in Aramaic, except perhaps for the more formal disputations when Hebrew would have been used. But all the Gospels are written in Greek and efforts to recover an Aramaic original from which the Greek translation was made have not been generally regarded by scholars as successful. The many quotations in the New Testament from the Old have been made from the Septuagint, as the Greek version is called, not from the Hebrew itself.

In such a situation it is likely that from the beginning the finer nuances of meaning may here and there have got blurred. The familiar word 'Lord', for instance, *Kyrios* in the Greek, was a polite word of everyday address, 'Sir'; it was also the word used in the Septuagint to render the most holy name of God, so holy that its original pronunciation is unknown, which the King James translators made into Jehovah; it was also used in the pagan Greek world as a title for the deities in mystery religions, as in the Lord Serapion; and it was a word increasingly favoured in the Roman Empire as a title for the Emperor. And when one reflects that *Kyrios* is one of the key Christian words, it is apparent that converts from different backgrounds would differ widely in the associations brought to their minds when they used it in worship.

But even had there been no difficulties of language (and, of course, the variations mentioned in the last paragraph carried possibilities of creative enrichment in their variety as well as of confusion), the Christian insistence that Jesus the Christ be worshipped as Lord and God had difficulties for the devout among both the Jews and Gentiles; and curiously enough, the difficulties for one were the opposite of the difficulties for the other.

To the Jew, the problem was monotheism: the primary belief fought for from the days of Sinai, defended with the blood of martyrs in Greek time, that there was only one God and that he alone could be worshipped. It was hard enough for the Jew to accept that Jesus had been the Messiah, for the Messiah was supposed to have been a God-supported victorious deliverer; whereas Jesus was an apparent failure who had died a degrading kind of death which showed, according to the Book Deuteronomy,[76] that he had been under God's curse. But even an accepted Messiah would not have been entitled to worship; worthy of all honours short of the divine though he would have been, he would have remained on the manward side of the unbridgeable gulf between Creator and creature.

It is most remarkable how quickly and how completely the early Christians associated Jesus in such an intimate way with God. Psychologically it is hard to decide whether a sturdy fisherman like Peter with the simple, conservative loyalties of his kind, or the subtle, highly trained, professional rabbi Saul with his inquisitor's temperament and commission, was the less likely to worship a contemporary co-religionist. Saul who became Paul certainly did so against all his inclinations.[77] No doubt all the Christian converts from Judaism (and that probably means a substantial majority of the first generation) would have replied, had they been challenged, that they did so because of a compulsion so strong they had to take it as divine; the better instructed of them would have added that their convictions were authenticated by a proper (again, the divine compulsion) reading of what the Scriptures foretold.

The compulsion in question was identified theologically as the compulsion of the Holy Spirit. Here we meet one of several ways in which the developing Hebrew experience of the living God had caused them almost unconsciously to modify without destroying their monotheism. God, who was complete in himself, moved among the order of creation in several overflows of energy of which His Spirit, who had 'moved over the face of the waters' to reduce to order the primeval chaos,[78] was the outstanding example. The Old Testament, and still more the literature produced between the Old Testament and the New, had described the experience of God acting within His creation under the form of many 'attributes'. Some of these, greatly used in the Psalms, are little more than poetic figures; we read of God's 'hand', His 'eyes', and so on. It is naïve to suppose, as some scholars in the past have done, that these figures of speech show that the Hebrews thought of God as an enormous human being; it is rather that their experience of Him was rather like being observed by an all-seeing eye or being protected by an outstretched hand.

But some of these 'attributes' of God were taken a great deal further. They cannot be described as acting independently of God; they were rather a matter of God's energies being deployed in certain well-marked ways. His 'Spirit', His 'Word', and His 'Wisdom' were three of the most important. It is important to realize that there is no question of a plurality of gods. But perhaps it was because the Hebrews' understanding of God as the Holy One, the Creator, so lofty and so all-embracing that nothing could exist outside His scope, was so much outside and 'beyond' the created order He was keeping in being, that their teachers and poets needed to some extent to personify God as He moved within His creation. They had to say that He was both utterly beyond and entirely within. Thus the Hebrews were able to go some way towards thinking of God as a unity which included a measure of inner differentiation.

Spirit, Word, and Wisdom. We are a long way still from the formal definitions of Christianity, of God as Three-in-One, as a Triunity of Father, Son, and Holy Spirit; but we have the raw materials for it. In particular we have the means used by Paul, the thoroughgoing orthodox rabbi, for associating Jesus so intimately with God. He identified Jesus with the Word and the Wisdom of God, sent forth as a Son to do his decisive and unique work of salvation. It is not clear how far St Paul had developed the inner differentiation of God's Unity into a definitive Trinity; he seems sometimes to write of the Spirit whom he so powerfully experienced as the Spirit of Christ and sometimes as the Spirit of God who pointed to Christ; it was in fact to be some time before that particular relationship was teased out into systematic form, and even now it can be misleading to attempt too great a degree of precision.

In one of his earliest letters, written so far as we know before he had developed the full sophistication of his letter to Colossae or of his circular letter of which the edition sent to Ephesus has survived, St Paul told the Galatians: '... When the time had fully come, God sent forth his Son, born of woman, born under the law, to redeem those who were under the law, so that we might receive adoption as sons.'[79] He was saying in his own idiom exactly the same thing as St John wrote in the stately words of his Gospel's opening chapter; and what both of them said was enough to enable the Jew who had been moved by the Spirit to find in Jesus the God-sent Saviour and to worship that same Jesus without forswearing his Jewish monotheism.

St Paul's use of the term 'God's Son' and St John's use of the term 'Word' would have been intelligible to both Jew and Gentile, though each might have understood the terms within a rather different range of thought. The main problem for the pagan was not the worship of another divine figure—he was used to an enormous number of divinities. Moreover, he was used to making identifications between the gods of one system and their equivalents in another. His problem was rather—if one can generalize over so varied a set of religious attitudes—that religion was above all deliverance from this world, from its transience, its materiality, its corruptibility. It was thus distasteful to hear of God coming into contact with the created order at all. There must surely be a number of intermediaries, of diminishing degrees of holiness, between the Supreme Power and the world. The pagan did not like the Jewish insistence on God as Creator. He preferred to think of some being a good deal lower in the hierarchical scale, soiling his hands by creating matter; a 'demiurge'. So the pagan's problem when he heard the Christian claims for Jesus was that Jesus had actually been born; that he had gone through the physical processes of human existence. He would much prefer his saviour to have been entirely spiritual, a spiritual visitor who would rescue the spiritual elements in mankind that were imprisoned in their fleshy tomb.

There were endless varieties of religious pagans in the world of the first century AD who thought broadly like that. Many of the words they used were very similar to the Christian words—spirit, word, wisdom, knowledge, perfection, son, among them. In some cases these words were derived from one or other of the current pagan philosophies; in some cases at second or third hand from the Judaism of the resident Greek communities; and in some cases from a mixture, perhaps worked up with elements from Egypt of elsewhere, into a regular cult. In certain cases converts who entered the Christian church from such a background had done too little to distinguish their new allegiance from their old one. Evidence of the subversive effects of such imperfectly converted converts is scattered widely throughout the New Testament: the vigorous means needed to counteract different types of deviation is particularly clear in St Paul's first letter to the Corinthians and his letter to the Colossians, where a debased Jewish influence was very strong; and in the first letter of St John. From the early second century various types of 'gnostic' sects followed the teaching of leaders who mostly took their starting point from some element of Christian teaching, but holding it in some way distorted by a total context such as has just been described. Until fairly recently such 'gnostic' (the term derives from their claim to a knowledge or 'gnosis' which made them superior to the common run of Christians) sects were open to investigation only through the writings of their opponents. Recent discoveries of ancient manuscripts have enabled scholars to study their teachings at first hand; perhaps the main change in perspective that has resulted comes from a fresh appreciation of the size of these groups. Whereas the general impression had been of a large, orthodox Christian centre with a number of small, uncertainly related splinter-groups, the picture is now of several large groups co-existing, one of which was seen in time to triumph as the orthodox catholic Church.[80]

The difficulties raised for the modern mind by the conviction that Jesus could only properly be treated as God stem from the domination of the empirical sciences. Our difficulties are very different from the ancient ones, whether Jewish or pagan. For the world into which the Christian gospel came was a world which was united in recognizing realms of existence beyond that of our present one. Jews, pagans, and Christians would all agree that there were divine powers outside and beyond our life, so they had no difficulty over the notion of a transcendent Being, however much they might differ over its nature and number. They would all agree that the divine life existed independently of ours, both before it and after it, so they would find no problem in the pre-existence of a divine Being should they admit the possibility that such a Being might so humble Himself as to enter human life. Nor, of course, would they have any difficulty over the survival of the human spirit into an existence fraught with awesome possibilities of bliss or of misery. And those three factors, the transcendence of God, the pre-existence of Christ, and the destiny of the human spirit to live beyond the limits of our present life, are three of the biggest problems the educated modern finds in accepting the traditional Christian faith in God the Father, the Son, and the Holy Spirit and in Jesus Christ who was that same Son living a human life, having been conceived into it by the Holy Ghost and born of the Virgin Mary. A fourth difficulty of a rather different order is that of particularity: why should that one life, lived in one place and at one period, in one religious tradition, be thought to have such far-reaching and indeed universal effect?

IX

The classical age of Christian theology lay between the fourth and the sixth centuries. It began with the emergence of the Church from an underground existence when the civil authorities in the person of the Emperor Constantine decided to halt the persecutions and to give the Church a legal and even a privileged existence. Councils of bishops were now able to meet and to decide which of the current formulations of the faith did best justice to the ancient traditions so tenaciously preserved through the difficult years that lay behind.

The conviction that Jesus must be treated as God meant that any statement of God's being must allow for the pre-existent Son to have been from the unimaginable start on a par with God; the catchphrase of the Alexandrian presbyter Arius, 'There was a time when he was not', was disallowed, though it was some time before the phrase of his chief opponent, Athanasius, 'being of one substance with the Father', was universally accepted. But once the Christian mind was clear that there existed in Jesus of Nazareth that which had from all eternity been one with God, the questions shifted to the manner in which God had united Himself with the man Jesus. In the language of dogmatic theology, the Trinitarian controversies were followed by the Christological.

It is fortunately not necessary for us to follow the tortuous discussions which ensued, where difficulties of language and of philosophical ambiguity were complicated by rivalries between the personalities of individual bishops, the rivalry of honour between their sees, and even nationalistic factors. All were agreed that Jesus was 'the Word made flesh'. Some stressed the human more, some the divine. Was the divinity as complete in the babe-in-arms as it was in the grown man, and if so, how? Was the incarnate Son of God equipped with all the divine knowledge, and if so had some part of his human equipment—mind? soul? spirit?—been replaced by the divine equivalent? Was it possible for his will as a human being to be at variance with his will as a 'member' of God? One reason why it is so hard to answer such teasing questions is that there are no universally agreed definitions over what constituted either humanness or divinity. The problems are with us still and anyone who would speak clearly about Jesus Christ cannot avoid making some practical decision about them.

The central thing that emerged from the early debates was that if Jesus was genuinely the Saviour, bringing together God and man, he must be both divine and human in such a way as to impair neither the divinity nor the humanity. On the one hand Jesus was not a good and holy man whom the Word came alongside and so controlled that his human will was completely at one with the divine. Such a view, that attributed to Nestorius of Antioch in the fifth-century controversies, 'really only makes our Lord different in degree, not in kind, from any really holy person', as a modern theologian has put it.[81] On the other hand he was not the semblance of a man who had been so fully taken over by God that his human nature had been effectively replaced by the divine, as some representatives of the rival school of Alexandrian theologians suggested.

The early Fathers reached the high point of their discussions at the Council of Chalcedon in 451. They produced there a definition which sought to express the balance between the human and the divine in such a way as to avoid the distortions shown when either the Antiochene stress on the human or the Alexandrian stress on the divine was allowed to predominate. Their statement, originally drawn up in Greek, has recently been retranslated as follows:[82]

> ... We ... confess our Lord Jesus Christ one and the same Son, the same perfect in Godhead, the same perfect in manhood, truly God and truly man, the same consisting of a reasonable soul and a body, of one substance with the Father as touching the Godhead, the same of one substance with us as touching the manhood, like us in all things apart from sin; begotten of the Father before all ages as touching the Godhead, the same in the last days for us and for our salvation, born from the Virgin Mary, the *Theotokos*, as touching the manhood, one and the same Christ, Son, Lord, Only-begotten, to be acknowledged in two natures, without confusion, without change, without division, without separation; the distinction of natures being in no way abolished because of the union, but rather the characteristic property of each nature being preserved, and concurring into one Person and one subsistence [in the Greek, *hypostasis*], not as if Christ were parted or divided into two persons, but one and the same Son and only-Begotten God, Word, Lord, Jesus Christ. ...

Subsequent theology has had many hard words to say of this definition and there have been many later attempts to define the Person of Christ. The real problem, as we indicated earlier, is to know what to make of the terms used. The proportions between

47

the terms have never been better put; and Christologies which have departed from them usually end up in a new version of one of the old inadequate statements which Chalcedon guards against. One particularly promising recent attempt to express the proportions of Chalcedon in modern language is that of Professor John Macquarrie.[83]

Of particular interest to our present inquiry is the Chalcedonian use of the term *Theotokos*. 'Mother of God', the usual English translation, is a phrase calculated to make Protestant hackles rise. It is a great pity that that is so, for it is not hard to understand the phrase in its true sense. It does not mean that the Virgin Mary is a goddess before whose birth-giving there was no god. 'The Fathers made bold to call the holy Virgin *Theotokos*', Cyril of Alexandria wrote to Nestorius who had objected to the phrase, 'not as though the nature of the Word or his godhead had its beginning from the holy Virgin, but forasmuch as his holy Body, endued with a rational soul, was born of her, to which Body also the Word was personally united, on this account he is said to have been born after the flesh.'[84] The phrases 'mother of the Lord', 'mother of the incarnate Word', 'mother of God Incarnate' can of course be used; but except for the last one, they could be used to suggest that Jesus was in some way less than God. The term 'mother of God' is primarily a statement not about her, but about her Son. Because her Son was who he was, there are indeed implications concerning her own person, which will be examined shortly. But in the first instance, the term is Christological, not Mariological.

An aspect of Mary's maternity which has caused particular difficulty to the modern mind has been the assertion that she gave birth to her Son while still a virgin, the child having had no human father. Attack on the doctrine has come from many sides. Only in two places in the New Testament is it mentioned, the Matthean and Lucan stories of the Annunciation, and in the first at least it looks as if it has been included to point to the fulfilment of a prophecy which may itself be the result of a mistranslation from Hebrew to Greek. Others have pointed to legends in ancient paganism of mysterious fatherings by the gods, and still others have connected it with a feeling that sexual encounter was intrinsically nasty and that therefore the birth of the Son of God by such means was not to be considered; the doctrine was in fact an early infiltration into

Christianity of the 'gnostic' tendency described earlier. Others again have attacked the doctrine from a general disbelief in miracles, only to be countered by strange stories of 'parthenogenesis' or virgin births in other areas of creation.

The doctrine and the pictures at the beginning of the two Gospels which underlie it seem admirably to indicate both the disjunction and the continuity between Christ and the rest of the human race; his 'otherness' as well as his 'brotherness', to return to our earlier informal terms. There is another and perhaps more profound way in which the doctrine enlarges our understanding of the Incarnation to the point where it is seen as a new departure in creation; we shall return to that in the final chapter. For the present, some words of John Macquarrie express the traditional belief in a modern philosophical idiom:

> Since an incarnation is to be understood precisely as the union of a being with Being in the fullest and most intimate way possible, ... then such an incarnation would be pre-eminently a work of the Holy Spirit. Such a union is conceivable only as one in which the initiative is from the side of Being, so that a doctrine of the virgin birth, in ascribing the initiative in incarnation to unitive Being (the Holy Spirit) is an appropriate symbol.[85]

X

'Protestants', wrote Cardinal Newman, 'have seldom any real perception of the doctrine of God and man in one person.'[86] He had in mind of course the Established Church of England of the early nineteenth century, so little occupied with doctrinal questions; and the pietistic or rationalist theology of Germany which was beginning to make itself felt. But when one looks at the more recent record of Protestant theology, one has to admit that there is still some truth in the assertion. It is particularly true of evangelical Anglican theology, in which there has been something of a revival since the Second World War. But, if published works are any guide, there has been little interest in the doctrine of Christ's person. In part it is because evangelicals are in such a hurry to expound the work of Christ, his atonement and the salvation it has brought, that they have little time to spare for what often seem to be 'preliminaries'. 'We are not commissioned as preachers of the gospel to tell men that because God the Son was born of Mary, there is fullness of life for all who share in His humanity. It is rather part of faithful and exclusive gospel witness to declare that, if Christ be not raised from the dead, our faith is vain, and we are yet in our sins'[87] expresses a prevalent attitude. Where there has been investigation of the nature of Christ's person, it has generally been in the interests of giving the authority of his divine person to a view of the infallibility of the Scriptures.

The fear that too much attention to Bethlehem will detract from saving attention to the cross and the empty tomb is closely connected with an anti-catholic spirit which has little time for the implications of Mary's role as *Theotokos*; with the consequence not only of serious impoverishment in the claiming of Christian privileges which we shall examine in later chapters, but also of an exaggerated and distorted emphasis on Christ's humanity. This is perhaps less a weakness of the neo-conservative evangelicals who have recently become such a force in the Church of England, than of more liberal protestants.

Again it is Cardinal Newman who, perhaps surprisingly, speaks for an 'evangelicalism' that keeps to the proportions of the Gospel and of the classical interpretation of its implications. He speaks of a 'range of thought' where Mary, not her Son, is the proper centre. 'If we placed our Lord in that centre, we should only be dragging Him from His throne, and making him an Arian kind of God; that is, no God at all.' He has in mind the range of experience which we may call creatureliness. 'Our Lord cannot pray for us, as a creature prays, as Mary prays; he cannot inspire those feelings which a creature inspires....'[88]

These words will seem strange to an evangelical, or to a liberal protestant brought up to view Jesus as our brother, as 'the man for others'. But it makes sense if one has reflected upon the 'otherness' of Jesus in the Gospels and in the claims made for him elsewhere in the New Testament. Certainly he is our Advocate, our High Priest, who has suffered and been tempted and so is able to help those who are tempted.[89] He has shared our experience, sin apart. But there are infinite tracts of his experience to which we must remain strangers. Leaving aside altogether his divinity, we do not know what it is like to experience the full glory of being completely human, as the Creator meant us to be, our fellowship with Him unbroken.

We cannot 'identify' fully with Jesus Christ. He remains the one who strides out ahead of his disciples, for whom the love and loyalty of the heart's devotion can never lose the awe due to one who is different in kind as well as in degree. But it is not so with Mary. She who gave him human birth is yet completely human. She is a sinner who is redeemed. It is with her that we may fully identify. It may be that for certain reasons due to her uniqueness as the mother of God she has reached the fullness of human potential sooner than the rest of us, but though she has made the journey more quickly she has still had the same path to tread, a path different from that of the sinless Saviour.

There is one particular range of thought, which has come into prominence since the time of Cardinal Newman, where faulty thinking about Christ has resulted from according him the central place properly due to his mother. That is the view, developed a century ago as a novelty, which has in this century passed into the unexpected presuppositions of many Christian people. Dr Mascall, the Anglican theologian who has done so much to clarify thought in this field, has expressed it thus:

> In the last century there was a great deal of liberal evolutionary Christology (not *only* in the last century—there has been a certain amount in this century too) which represented our Lord as the climax to which the human race was brought by God's working within—and nothing more. Now that is not true of our Lord; but it is true about his Mother; she is the greatest thing that the human race could produce through the grace of God working within. But when she had been produced, then the working of God from within was met by the act of God from without. The divine Word himself comes upon Mary and in her womb takes human nature: there the working of God from within is met by the act of God from without. *That* was the preparation for *this*.[90]

It was a preparation undertaken in conditions of great particularity. It is interesting to read again the opening chapters of St Luke's Gospel. The characters one meets are of a very particular kind: Zechariah, Elizabeth, Joseph, Mary, Simeon, Anna; they could hardly be more different from the successful ecclesiastics in those days of the Roman occupation of the Holy Land, Annas and Caiaphas; nor from the learned and respected rabbis, Gamaliel and Saul. They were humble, unobtrusive, insignificant, perhaps ineffectual people. Yet they were the 'poor' of the Lord whom the psalmists realized to be especially blessed, and they were those who, at the psychological moment of God's plans for the world's redemption, were 'looking for the consolation of Israel'.[91] They were the 'faithful remnant of Israel', the ones for whom the whole mighty story of the Old Testament had been a preparation. And of that circle of the Lord's chosen poor it was a young girl who was singled out for the greatest burden and the greatest privilege which ever fell to the lot of a human being—to be the human mother of the eternal Word of God. She was chosen, but the dialogue in St Luke's account shows that her own response was not a foregone conclusion. She asked for clarifications and she was given them. 'And Mary said, "Behold, I am the handmaid of the Lord; let it be to me according to your word." '[92] Mary exercised her free choice to accept God's choice of her; and with that action the whole long story of Israel's chosenness to be God's special people among all the nations of the world was vindicated.

Theotokos was in the first instance a Christological, not a Mariological, term; but its secondary significance was very definitely Mariological and it is hard to see how any Christian theology can be genuinely evangelical without doing justice to it. We may end this chapter with two quotations from English poetry, one from the nineteenth century and one medieval:

> The zone where two glad worlds for ever meet,
> Beneath that bosom ran;
> Deep in that womb the conquering Paraclete
> Smote Godhead on to man.[93]

> Mother and maiden
> Was never such as she;
> Well may such a lady
> God's mother be.[94]

3
Mary Among Her Son's People

I MOTHER AND DISCIPLE

'Blessed are you among women, and blessed is the fruit of your womb', exclaimed Elizabeth, filled with the Holy Spirit, when her young cousin Mary visited her.[1] A careful scrutiny of St Luke's presentation[2] showed that Mary's blessedness was not merely in the physical fact of her childbearing; it was involved with her belief in the Word of God, and with her obedience in carrying out that Word as she heard it. The mother had to become a disciple; and her discipleship was a fulfilment of Simeon's prophecy[3] that a sword would pierce her own soul. Mary was not only the mother of her Son: she was one of her Son's people.

St Luke continues the theme in the second volume of his book, which we know as The Acts of the Apostles. To understand the picture we must look again at the writer's theological pattern. Some commentators on the Acts (as we may call it for short) have stressed the phrase in the opening paragraph where the author refers to his first book, which described 'all that Jesus began to do and to teach'.[4] The second volume is the continuation. It might perhaps be known for a truer summary of its contents as 'the acts of the ascended Christ through the Holy Spirit, by the intermediary of certain apostles'. The pattern of God's action seen in the earthly life of Jesus is continued in the early Church, the assembly of his followers.

The similarity of pattern which St Luke wishes to show in the events concerning Jesus earthly and Jesus heavenly extends to his literary method; and especially is this so in the preliminary sections which in both volumes precede the main events, and to a large extent set the main emphases within which they will be described. The first chapter of the Gospel brought before the reader a number of people who were living in expectancy of the Messiah's coming, a faithful remnant of the people of the Old Covenant in whose midst the Kingdom was to be established in power. The first chapter

53

of the Acts shows the risen Lord teaching his apostles about the Kingdom. When these apostles asked him about the timing of future events, he answered most indirectly (thereby correcting the error in their questions), promising them the power they needed to be his witnesses 'to the end of the earth'.[5]

As in the opening sections of the Gospel, the preliminary affairs in the Acts succeed one another in a series of connected 'snapshots'. The commission to be witnesses and the promise of necessary power is followed by that disappearance of the Lord from human sight which we call Ascension. The disciples then returned to Jerusalem, where they established themselves in 'the upper room'; a sizeable one, presumably, since St Luke lists twelve people by name and probably includes another half-dozen at least.[6] Evidently they did not stay constantly in that upper room, for in the presence of about 120 people Peter presided over the casting of lots which resulted in the choice of Matthias to replace the traitor Judas.[7]

The function of the group in the upper room was all-important. They all 'with one accord devoted themselves to prayer'.[8] The inner power group of the incipient movement, in fact; and their names are therefore particularly significant: the eleven apostles St Luke has named in the first volume[9] without, of course, the deceased traitor; 'together with the women and Mary the mother of Jesus, and with his brothers'.

It is significant that Mary was named among those devoting themselves to prayer. It is significant also that St Luke does not mention her again. Her task was essentially the historical role of having borne the Christ;[10] any further contribution she had to make was a theological consequence of that supreme fact. The Book of Acts is concerned with the phase in the operations of God which resulted from the redemptive incarnation of his Son. Mary's presence in the waiting church at the start of the Acts of the Apostles, however, is a reminder that the birth of the Redeemer was the birth of a genuinely human being. Just as motherhood does not end when the child is born, so the mother through whom the Christ was born was not shed at his maturity as a spent rocket is shed from a spacecraft. But whereas in St Luke's first volume she had been the star of the prologue, she had no speaking part in the second. The mother through whom the more-than-davidic king had been born had become the disciple within the Kingdom.

There has been no more acute appreciation of the Virgin's situation, nor one more strikingly expressed, than in the line which begins Dante's magnificent final canto of the *Paradiso: Vergine madre, figlia del tuo figlio*, 'Virgin mother, daughter of your Son'. The prayer which Dante thus puts into the mouth of St Bernard conveys with the greatest possible precision the paradox of the Lord's mother: after the order of nature, his mother; after the order of grace, the daughter of her own Son. If we are to understand the position which Mary rightfully holds among her Son's people, we must do justice to both sides of that paradox.[11]

It is at this point that the rather perplexing evidence from the fourth Gospel comes clearer. It is notoriously difficult to know how to interpret St John. His presentation of Jesus seems to move at more than one level. There are so many indications of eyewitness and direct memory that the determination to see it as a theological reflection by the second generation upon the experiences of the first does not seem as compelling as on other grounds it should. Yet in no sense is the Gospel a mere chronicle. More than with any of the other three, the fourth Gospel seems to present the earliest events in the light of the whole story. Perhaps it is safest to see it as a retelling of the apostolic experience in the light of later events, a reinterpretation which is seen as the fulfilment of an earlier promise.[12] Here, if anywhere, the events are to be seen with the insight of the Holy Spirit.

Two incidents only are involved. The first is the strangely disturbing one at the wedding feast at Cana, where Jesus and his mother were both among the guests. 'When the wine gave out, the mother of Jesus said to him, "They have no wine." And Jesus said to her, "O woman, what have you to do with me? My hour has not yet come." His mother said to the servants, "Do whatever he says to you."' The result, of course, was the unlimited supply of wine which flowed from the jars used for purification rites. The writer underlines the significance of the incident by situating it in a series: 'This, the first of his signs, Jesus did in Cana of Galilee, and manifested his glory; and his disciples believed in him.'[13]

There is no need to spend time on the apparently brusque form of address which Jesus used to his mother. It implied no discourtesy. It is important to read the incident in the theological context; the first of a series of signs where Jesus shows for those with eyes to see, his true inner nature, his 'glory'. In this instance it is probably correct to see the main thrust of meaning in the superiority, in quantity as well as in quality, of the wine which, at Jesus's bidding, came out of the purification jars. The new life which Jesus was to bring was that much fuller and more generous than the life of the Judaism of which he was the fulfiller. The six subsequent 'signs' which the writer indicates in a similar manner from among the many incidents in the Gospel extend this fundamental point, showing how it works out in situations of mounting human crisis, the climax being the raising of Lazarus from the dead.[14]

Only within this theological framework may we properly understand the exchange between Jesus and his mother. She clearly has an important part in the incident; her presence was not accidental to the meaning St John wishes to convey. His mother believes in Jesus at least to the extent of knowing him to be the person to turn to in an embarrassing situation. He answers her in a virtually untranslatable phrase, fortunately rescued from obscurity by his own explanation: 'My hour has not yet come.' Undaunted by any rebuff, she then tells the servants to do whatever he told them. The result was a manifestation of his glory in the supply of need; and the consequence was that 'his disciples believed in him'. A point of some interest, in view of what we saw from St Luke's picture, was that his mother showed herself to be a disciple while the disciples still needed in some measure to have their belief confirmed.

Of greater importance is the statement that the 'hour' of Jesus had not yet come. Similar phrases, from the lips of Jesus or from the evangelist's comment, make it clear that the 'hour' arrived when Jesus engaged in decisive victorious combat with the forces of darkness; that is, the hour of his death with its surprising reversal by resurrection.[15] It was as that hour struck that St John again brings the Lord's mother conspicuously to our notice. The soldiers had crucified Jesus and diced for possession of his tunic. 'But standing by the cross of Jesus were his mother, and his mother's sister, Mary the wife of Clopas, and Mary Magdalene. When Jesus saw his mother, and the disciple whom he loved standing near, he said to his mother, "Woman, behold your son!" Then he said to the disciple, "Behold your mother!" And from that hour the disciple took her to his own home.'[16]

It seems congruous with St John's method as an evangelist, his habit of describing events so as to show two or more layers of meaning simultaneously expressed by the same event, to read into this episode more than a good son's care for his mother's future when he is no longer there to provide for her. The contrast between his attitude towards his mother on this occasion, when his 'hour' was upon him, and his attitude to her at Cana, when his hour had not yet come, lends support to those commentators who see here the symbolic birth of the Church, born from the cross. Mary and 'the disciple whom Jesus loved' are the first of the new community; a community whose internal relationships are to be marked by mutual care. We leave for discussion later the question of whether the particular incident supports the general principle that all disciples are to look upon the Lord's mother as their mother and to receive from her a mother's care.

II 'MOST HIGHLY FAVOURED LADY'

The mother of Jesus was her Son's disciple. In this chapter we shall see what this simple statement implies, to what extent Mary's discipleship is something which she shares in common with all true disciples, and to what extent it is something which no one else can share.

We have followed out the descriptions of discipleship in the New Testament references to Mary. It was clear from St Luke that discipleship was largely a matter of hearing the Word of God and doing it. Such discipleship was bound to be costly. It was further made plain that while discipleship was a matter of learning from Jesus, and so required personal decision, it was a way of life to be worked out in association with other people, notably with fellow-disciples; although deep attachment in loyalty and devotion to the master were likely to be involved, discipleship to Jesus was no matter of exclusive affection. Discipleship meant association in a kingdom, a family, a church (in the basic sense of the Greek *ekklesia*, a group of people who have been 'called out'). St John makes this point particularly clear in the words which the crucified Jesus spoke to his mother and the disciple.

Those words from the cross stress another point about disciple-ship, which is also clear from St Luke; that the disciple's choice of Jesus as master to learn from is only a part of the truth. There is also the master's choice of the disciple to whom the teaching is offered. It is interesting to examine the many encounters in the Gospels and the Acts where discipleship is either accepted or re-jected, noting on which party the emphasis is placed. There were many short-term disciples who listened for a while and then for some reason or other found the going too hard. The disciple who perseveres seems often to be the disciple who has been in-vited.

Discipleship is a pictorial, dramatic word much used in the Gospels. It is far less common elsewhere in the New Testament, per-haps because it refers properly to one part only of Christian existence, that of learning. It is too imprecise for understanding and explain-ing the deeper dynamics of God's action in calling human beings into positive relationship with Himself. Unfortunately, the more technical words salvation, election, grace, and faith, have proved to be particularly divisive between the various Christian traditions; in fact, a cynic might say that the more capable of precision a theological term, the more it serves to separate Christians.

'Grace' is the classic example. The theological word 'grace' means the undeserved favour which God bestows on human beings in their state of sin, or estrangement from Him. In the writings of St Paul, 'grace' is one of the key categories for understanding God's action on behalf of sinful man; but as the apostle writes of it, grace is in no way abstract, or confined to the outside. Grace is something which St Paul experienced, and which he writes about as to people who have experienced it too. 'You know the grace of our Lord Jesus Christ,' he could write,[17] 'that though he was rich, yet for your sake he became poor, so that by his poverty you might become rich.' Grace in fact is a way of describing God's love, in particular as it is directed to ending the basic human disaster. 'God shows his love to us in that while we were yet sinners Christ died for us.'[18] And the emphasis was by no means a peculiarity of St Paul extrapolating doctrine from his vivid personal experience. For St John can write: 'In this is love, not that we loved God but that he loved us and sent his Son to be the expiation for our sins'.[19] An essential point wherever the truth of grace is presented, is that it is God moving out into action quite regardless of human deserving. God takes the initiative, grace takes priority. Human excellence, moral goodness, perceptiveness, even faith itself, are irrelevant to the appearance of grace, however much they may result from it. Thus St Paul can write in one of the great Christian passages, as profound as it is incisive: 'By grace have you been saved through faith; and this is not your own doing, it is the gift of God—not because of works, lest any man should boast. For we are his workmanship, created in Christ Jesus for good works, which God prepared beforehand, that we should walk in them.'[20]

The experience of grace is the common property of Christians. Indeed, the fact of grace (whether 'experienced' in a personal sense or not) is that which constitutes a Christian, someone whose approach to God is made not on his own merits but on God's acceptance and welcome. The Church is the community of those whose fundamental relationship with God is based on the relationship which God has established with them; and the Holy Spirit in the Church as a body and in its members as individuals creates an awareness of what God is and of what they are, with the consequent fruit of changed dispositions.[21] There is a subtle interplay between the individual and the corporate which is hard to express, for in human experience uncontrolled by the Spirit the two are often opposed. One of the most obvious effects of the Spirit's operation is so to reconcile this opposition that the individual is no longer constrained to assert his individuality over against the group; which in its turn is coherent and secure enough to allow the individual to develop within its fold. The fact of continuing sin often frustrates the full extent of the Spirit's work, but never to the point of extinguishing it: the gates of hell do not prevail.

It is encouraging to find that the church at Corinth, so ridden by factions, was the one to which St Paul wrote most fully about the Spirit.[22] Apart from the main study of his work in that letter, St Paul applies the teaching in two phrases which when read side by side bring out the interplay between individual and corporate. Writing about the rival groups in the Corinthian church, he says to the lot of them: 'Do you not know that you are God's temple and that God's Spirit dwells in you? If anyone destroys God's temple, God will destroy him. For God's temple is holy, and that temple

59

[singular] you [plural] are.'[23] Writing about sexual immorality, he stresses the individual indwelling of the Spirit. 'Do you not know that your body is a temple of the Holy Spirit within you, which you have from God? You are not your own; you were bought with a price. So glorify God in your body.'[24]

The Christian gospel does not end therefore with the reconciliation of sinful men to God. It begins with an offer to put people in the clear with Him as the start of a process where they become in accomplished fact what in His purpose He has already declared them to be. Neither in the declaration nor in the becoming is it a matter primarily of their own excellence but rather of the divine initiative of grace. God in His Spirit moves into human life and into human lives to confront them with the fact of Christ, His Son and their Saviour. From first to last salvation is from God. This basic, biblical Christian truth was and is the great theme of evangelical religion. 'It is beyond doubt that the century of the Reformation needed to be recalled to an understanding of God as God', wrote Donal Flanagan. It needed to have a clear emphasis placed on salvation as of God, not of man. 'It needed to have a clear distinction made between the word of God and the words of man. It needed to realize once more how far the human element can adulterate the gospel as this is understood and lived in the world.'[25] But he adds: 'Their commitment to try to keep God's salvation from contamination seems to have carried them as far as a certain refusal of the human which cannot be justified. On the other hand Roman Catholics have in their doctrines about Mary committed themselves clearly to an affirmation of the human as God's creation and the mode and vehicle of his salvation.'

Dr Flanagan thus takes up positively the point which Protestant theologians attack as the most dangerous aspect of Mariological developments. Professor David L. Wells, for example, quotes with approval the dictum of Karl Barth that '... The "mother of God" of Roman Catholic Marian dogma is simply the principle, type, and essence of the human creature co-operating servant-like (*ministerialiter*) in its own redemption on the basis of prevenient grace....' and adds his own gloss: 'Mary is the prototype of the Roman Catholic. By her co-operative action, she won the approval of God....'[26] Philip E. Hughes also sees Mariology as the 'logical outworking of the Roman Catholic doctrine of grace',[27] where '... Salvation has become jointly the work of both God and man.' We are back at the theological heart of the Protestant's sense of outrage; for, Hughes goes on, 'To conceive of salvation in these terms inevitably detracts from the fullness of the grace of God in Christ Jesus. It renders that grace inadequate and demands its supplementation. And it detracts from the glory that is due solely to God, dividing that glory between God and a creature.'[28]

But does it? Dr Flanagan, who has clearly worked through such serious objections seriously, thinks otherwise. And the decision of the Second Vatican Council to 'situate' its teaching on Mary 'in the Mystery of Christ and the Church'[29] shows a determination on the part of the authorities of his Church to submit the matter to biblical control; and even if we do not find that control always exercised successfully,[30] it will certainly be worth while to open the question again. We must of course admit that there is much in popular practice and no doubt in everyday Catholic teaching which needs such control as badly now as it did, Dr Flanagan agrees, at the time of the Reformation; but similar complaints would no doubt follow a scrutiny of any actual Christian church. One important question to ask is whether Catholic Mariology does in fact detract from the glory that is due solely to God; we may look afresh at the Scriptures to see whether perhaps the division of glory between God and a creature is being made in the proportions which are agreeable to God's Word. In doing so we shall be carrying out not only what the Catholic Dr Flanagan wants done, but also answering a part of the Protestant Professor Atkinson's plea for a new look at the possibilities which existed before the Council of Trent (as he understands it) so tragically shackled itself by its anti-Protestant commitment.[31]

It is interesting that Dr Flanagan wishes the task to figure on the theological agenda of his own Church. In particular he wants to see Marian doctrine developed in relation to the human, and to the work of the Spirit. It is perhaps impertinent for a Protestant to join in a discussion among Catholics; but the title of Dr Flanagan's paper was 'An Ecumenical Future for Roman Catholic Theology of Mary'; and the terms in which he invites discussion must be of interest to all serious Christian thinkers.

We have now established a context of thought in which to return to the consideration of the Lord's mother. We saw in the last chapter how clearly as well as economically St Luke showed her place in the Church as it awaited the Spirit's empowering. The mother was also the disciple. We may now look again at those passages at the start of his Gospel where St Luke shows how she became the mother; and we shall see that the motherhood was itself an expression of discipleship.

Mary might be taken as the prototype of the human being who has received grace. The angel of the Annunciation greeted her with words of profoundly theological import: 'Hail, O favoured one, the Lord is with you!'[32] Whatever the additional meanings in the phrase generally translated 'full of grace', the primary one is clear; it is 'who has received grace' and as such might be applied to any Christian. There are unique features about the Lord's mother which we shall consider shortly. But they are special conditions which are held within a framework shared by all human beings to whom God, in Christ, has made himself known and perhaps potentially by all human beings whatever.

Mary is also the prototype of the human being who is invited to respond to the grace received. The point is so important that we must give it some space. Grace is an invitation into personal relationship, into mutuality. Grace is not compulsion—the term 'irresistible grace' may have a proper sense but the implications of its everyday meaning are most misleading. Grace makes sons, not slaves; lovers, not clients. Grace does not humiliate; it makes possible the dignity of humility. Grace does not pauperize[33] even though it supplies everything. In a word, grace constitutes the fully human.

The free agency of man is a cardinal truth accepted by the whole Church. We all free to accept or reject God's plan for us. The whole Bible proves this. Mary is no exception to the rule. Mary might have refused.... The angel Gabriel was sent, not only to make the annunciation, but to gain Mary's concurrence or consent, to fall in with God's will.

The devotional address from which those words were taken was given not by a Catholic, but by the daughter of General Booth of the Salvation Army who headed up the work in France and was known as the Maréchale; and it was issued with a warm commendation from Handley Moule, the famous evangelical Bishop of Durham at the turn of the century.[34]

Dr John V. Taylor, Bishop of Winchester and former General Secretary of the Church Missionary Society,[35] and the author of one of the most distinguished volumes in the Christian Foundations series, *For All the World*, has written on this theme with great power and insight in the revised version of his Edward Cadbury lectures published under the title *The Go-Between God*.[36] The book is clearly one which makes a big contribution to the themes of the human and of the Holy Spirit, and of the interrelations of the two. An examination of the theology of mission, the first half of the book deals with the 'facts of life', the second half with the 'style of life'. The 'facts' considered are: Annunciation, Conception, Gestation, Labour, Birth, and Breath. By 'annunciation' Dr Taylor means experiences, not necessarily religious, whose core is the mutual recognition of two parties in an encounter where one is the 'seer' and one the 'seen'. 'I have in mind', he writes, 'several renaissance pictures of St Luke's story which emphasize the mutually enraptured gaze of the angel and the Virgin' (one of the plates in the book is a reproduction of Franciabigio's *Annunciation* in the Uffizi Gallery at Florence) 'and the dove-symbol of the Holy Spirit spinning, as it were, the thread of attention between them.' He quotes poems by Edwin Muir and Rilke (the latter in N. K. Cruikshank's translation) which place this experience most precisely.

'I have quoted these meditations on a familiar story', Dr Taylor comments,

not to turn the discussion into a 'religious' channel, but because they describe so clearly the kind of seeing I am talking about. I am not thinking of what is narrowly described as 'encounter with God', but of quite unreligious commonplace experiences. And if we try to remember them more carefully, I think we shall notice that what happens is this. The mountain or tree I am looking at ceases to be merely an object I am observing and becomes a subject, existing in its own life, and saying something to me—one could almost say *nodding* to me in a private conspiracy. That, in fact, is the precise meaning of the word 'numinous', which comes from the Latin *nuo*, to nod or beckon. The truly numinous experience is not marked only by primitive awe in the face of the unknown or overwhelming, but occurs also when something as ordinary as a sleeping child, as simple and objective as a flower, suddenly *commands* attention.

There are actually two stages in my experience. First, I am forced to recognize the real *otherness* of what I am looking at: it does not depend on my seeing or responding; it exists without me. And, second, there is a *communication* between us which I am bound to admit, if I am not obstinately blind, has not entirely originated in myself....[37]

Dr Taylor insists that the annunciation experience belongs to the human condition, not merely to the religious human or even to the specifically Christian human. He does so, not from a wish to identify the divine with the human 'without remainder',[38] but from his deep conviction of the unity between creation and redemption. He quotes a great deal from human creators and their work—poets, artists, scientists; those in fact whose perception takes them to the margins of experience and discloses to them and to others through them the patterns and the connections which we so often either fail to see or else take for granted.

The Annunciation of the Messiah's birth may therefore be seen as a very special instance of a basically human experience. What was true of the approach of grace and the invitation to respond was true also of the response made: Mary's 'Let it be to me according to your word.' The choice, acceptance or refusal, is a genuine possibility. Once more John Taylor is helpful. Under the heading of 'Conception' he reviews some 'frontier' thinking from academic scientists, especially in the field of biology, which implies that 'spontaneity and choice are at least as important as chance through the whole physical structure of the universe. It is certain that choice plays increasingly the greater part as life advances from lower to higher forms. With the appearance of human reason, choice consciously takes over from chance the direction of the evolutionary process.'[39] Mary's choice was therefore an indication of her developed humanity. Furthermore, her choice involved her in considerable risk; but then, as once more Dr Taylor makes clear, risk on behalf of others, the actual put in jeopardy for the sake of the potential, may be seen (by those who follow the clue provided for us, 'when the Creator Spirit at the heart of all being emerged

64

incarnate in the manhood of Jesus ...') as a basic principle of creativity. It 'can best be summed up in the word "sacrifice" '.[40]

Mary was indeed a 'most highly favoured lady'; and the favour she received was in the first place that of being so fully human in her response when the gracious Spirit approached her.

III

The uniqueness of Mary's motherhood lay not in the fact that she was a mother, nor that she was a virgin mother, but that she was the mother of God; that is, it was a uniqueness derived from her Son. Anything in her position which is not shared in all human motherhood is reflected back from him.

In an earlier chapter[41] we approached the matter by following out the statement in the Creed, 'conceived by the Holy Spirit, born of the Virgin Mary', a phrase which emphasizes both the continuity and the discontinuity of the One who was born. Language and concepts are inadequate to express an event with which there is strictly no comparison. Yet the traditional language has as its weakness the suggestion that the Son came as a visitor from outside. The transcendental way of speaking needs correction by another which stresses that the One being incarnated was already present as the Creator within his creation; for he is One in whom all things consist. The thought of Jesus as the Lord breaking in from outside needs to be balanced by the understanding of his arrival as emerging. To quote John Taylor again: 'The child that was born that night in the city of David on the eve of the census was no exception' to the common heredity of mankind. 'What broke surface then was not simply the sum total of all that had been, but its cause; not the surging processes of creation alone, but creativity itself. We call Mary's child "Emmanuel" because we see in him the God who has always been with us, always in the midst. There is no need for him to intervene as a stranger from an outside world. He is already here.'[42]

The understanding of Jesus as emerging rather than as breaking in from outside is deeply rooted in the biblical view; Taylor cites St John: 'All that came to be was alive with his life, and that life was the light of men.... He was in the world; but the world, though it owed its being to him, did not recognize him. He entered into his own realm, and his own would not receive him.'[43] 'What we see in Jesus', Dr Taylor concludes, 'is the Creator Spirit, the activator of all being, focused entirely into one human spirit. Or, looking at it the other way round, we see manhood completely surrendered to, and possessed by, the Spirit of God.'[44] If we are to speak at all adequately of the mother of Jesus the Lord, we must have in mind these two complementary ways of looking at him. For, as Dr Taylor rightly says, in him we see the new kind of man. 'This is ... the next unimaginable step forward which man had to take in obedience of the lure of the unfulfilled. But inasmuch as man never could or never would take that step, the God who always works from inside the processes took the step for him, as a man.' 'For all we know,' Dr Taylor adds in a thought-provoking aside, 'that may have been how every previous "step" was taken.'[45]

What then of her, whose womb was the site of such a momentous event? What manner of woman could have stood such strain? To think of Jesus as the Spirit who brooded over the face of the waters, the power at the heart of the developing creation, now emerging into human life as the incarnate Word, throws more, not less, importance on the one who gave him birth. It renders obviously impossible the old view, just tenable if the Incarnation is regarded exclusively as invasion, that she was an instrument through which her Son passed, a mere temporary 'host' who provided birth-giving facilities. The 'emergent' picture stresses the solidarity with the humanity to which he belongs and which he transcends. We are back at the importance of the milieu to which Mary belonged; the humble, insignificant people around the Temple in whom the expectation still burned that God would once more rise to deliver his chosen ones. Those people, incredible as it must have seemed to the worldly-wise Sadducean establishment, were the 'faithful remnant of Israel'; and, incredible as it seems to our modern sophistication, they made up the tiny segment of humanity from which the creative Word and Spirit were to break surface in Jesus, and through his life, debate, and resurrection achieve the greatest step ever made in creation, the New Man. And in that circle of the truly humble, so bright with the light of faith and hope, the brightest of all was a young girl called Mary.

It is time to return to the Catholic insistence on human perfectibility. 'There is an insidious temptation to view the human as

perfect in Jesus Christ and somehow corrupt in all its other mani-
festations. This', declares Dr Flanagan, 'is not the message of
the triumph of creation.'[46] 'Mary', declares Professor Wells, 'is the
prototype of the Roman Catholic. By her co-operative action, she
won the approval of God.'[47]

A way through the seemingly total barrier between those two
views may open up from the implications of the Protestant professor's choice of words. Why should it be supposed that Mary's
co-operation 'won God's approval'? The sequence of events in St
Luke's account suggests that God's approval, in so far as that is
relevant, preceded Mary's choice of obedience; she was highly
favoured before she declared herself the handmaid of the Lord. But
to speak of 'approval' is to intrude a note of moral approbation or
disapprobation too prominently into the situation. 'Natural man',
writes Dr Taylor, 'seems to grow up with a desperate need to be
approved of';[48] and the religion of the Pharisees, like most religious
systems, offered a means of satisfying that need. St Paul, of course,
felt an overwhelming intensity of that need, and the force of the ex-
plosion triggered off by his discovery that after all Judaism did not
supply it, coloured his whole subsequent life and thought. No rules
ever framed, indeed, will satisfy the need more than by just masking
it; for that is not their function. The answer which was revealed to
St Paul, and which was later to be rediscovered by earnest men all
down the ages, was that rules had no bearing on the deepest needs
of man. Jesus scandalized his contemporaries by such declarations
as, 'Your Heavenly Father makes his sun to rise on the good and
bad alike',[49] and generally deflated the professionally righteous.

Evangelical Christians make much of sin as a barrier between
God and man which only God can breach. They are right to do so
and Christians of other traditions often stand properly rebuked.
But they are wrong in their often unspoken assumption that sin
is to be described in moral terms. Their error lies partly in mistaking
the symptoms for the disease; and partly in supposing that the first
stage in rehabilitation is the final goal. Sin may be defined com-
prehensively as whatever in man frustrates the purpose of God.
Sin thus severs that fellowship with God for which man was created,
the joy in God, and so on. Sin may be rebellion, it may be a falling
short. It is always a contrast between the actual and the potential,
so it is a falling short of what might be. And it is always a matter

of living by some self-chosen code (even one with excellent credentials in the Scriptures) instead of in surrender to the Holy Spirit, so
it is rebellion. God in Christ overcame it in both aspects, giving
himself up to small men who fell short of their potential by living
according to their code and could not tolerate the continued existence of him who seemed to flaunt it. He bore their evil and with it
the evil of mankind of which they were a representative sample,
letting it do its worst to him and overcoming it by the completeness
of his reliance upon the Spirit. And so, because Jesus has taken
away the sin of the world, the way is open for all human beings to
connect with God in such a way that their own potential in his
purpose may be fulfilled.

Mary, to return to Professor Wells's dictum, is not merely the
prototype of the Roman Catholic. She is the prototype of the whole
human race. We shall return to the implications of that statement
later. For the moment, we may concentrate on what the Roman
Catholic Church calls her Immaculate Conception.

' ... the Blessed Virgin Mary, at the first instant of her Conception, by a singular privilege and grace of the omnipotent God, in
consideration of the merits of Jesus Christ, the Saviour of mankind,
was preserved free from all stain of original sin. ...' So ran Pope
Pius IX's Dogmatic Definition of 1854.[50] Since then the belief has
been binding upon Catholics. It is not in the same way a part of
Eastern Orthodox dogma, though most Orthodox would accept
its substance. But the context of thought about original and actual
sin is strange to the Eastern Christian mind; and of course that papal
authority with which it was proclaimed as a dogma of the Church
is not acceptable to them.

The Protestant world, apart from the section of the Anglo-
Catholic movement which had a yearning for papal infallibility,
received it coldly. It was couched in those juridical terms which so
often insulated official Roman Catholicism from being understood
at any depth by other Christians; and its lack of any obvious
scriptural support made it seem an unnecessary excrescence upon
the faith. It was also frequently misunderstood, being seen as a
counterpart to the Virgin Birth of Christ and a part of the Roman
tendency to assimilate to the mother the virtues of her Son. Thus
Bishop Langton Fox was constrained in the opening paragraph of
his pamphlet on the doctrine to insist that it 'does not refer to the

moment when our Lady conceived our Blessed Lord, but to the moment in which she herself was conceived by her mother, St Anne. Nor does it suggest that Mary's coming into being was physically in any way an exception to the laws of nature.[51] To say, therefore, as Dr Wells does, 'Like Christ, Mary was conceived without sin....',[52] is misleading.

It is misleading because it might suggest that Mary, like her Son, had no need of a Saviour. The birth of Mary was attended by none of the discontinuity which we saw in the birth of Jesus, safeguarded there for Christian thought in the doctrine of the Virgin Birth. Mary, who rejoiced in her Saviour, was the last person to have no need of one. The doctrine of the Immaculate Conception does not suggest that, in herself, Mary was sinless. It was not her merits but those of her Son which were, so to speak, applied to her in advance. As much as any other Christian she was saved by the blood of Jesus.

Bishop Fox devotes much of his pamphlet to showing how suitable it was for Mary to have been preserved from the start from original as well as from actual sin, or rather, how unsuitable it would have been for her to have been contaminated. '... How could Mary be said to have been made fit to stand in the relationship of Mother to the all-pure God if the devil could claim, and claim truly, that once, even if only for a moment, she had been in the state of Original sin? ... Every mind that has even the vaguest appreciation of the repugnance of God to sin will see at once that God would preserve His Mother from even Original sin.'[53] He has earlier made it clear that God would preserve her from actual sin.

Bishop Fox is of course writing a popular tract for Roman Catholics. He asserts, without spending time establishing them, the traditional Catholic teachings on the two kinds of sin and the connection between them. Actual sin is 'any thought, word, or action against the law of God'. Original sin was that of Adam which, through the solidarity of the human race has 'committed' all mankind 'to a condition which is displeasing to God'.[54] The displeasing condition is seen in the lack of gifts higher than the natural which were the Creator's intention for mankind, notably a share in God's own life. All human beings are therefore 'like people who are descendants of a man once honoured, favoured, and made wealthy by his king, but who find themselves born in poverty and without honour or favour, because their ancestor turned traitor'. The analogy is clearly one to open up embarrassing questions and Bishop Fox is at some pains to show how Mary (or anyone else subject to original sin) could be held responsible for it, and why Mary therefore needed exemption from it.

The Anglo-Catholic theologian Dr E. L. Mascall treats the subject differently, for he was writing (or rather speaking) to a basically learned society, and what is more in the context of debate with the Eastern Orthodox. He stresses the antiquity of the view that, whether or not Mary was conceived without original sin, she was in fact completely free from it at her birth. The Franciscans in the medieval debates held the specific teaching, the Thomists opposed it; her sinlessness was agreed. 'The point at issue was simply whether the grace which is normally conferred by baptism was given to her at the moment of her conception or while she was still in her mother's womb.'[55] Dr Mascall then makes a statement which would ease Bishop Fox's problem in popular communication: 'And if there is any intellectual difficulty in the matter, I must say that it seems to me easier to believe in Mary's freedom from original than from actual sin.' 'To suppose that Mary was free from actual sin without having received any special grace at her creation', Dr Mascall continues later in his exposition, 'would seem to me to be very difficult and in fact to place an almost impossible burden upon human free will.'[56]

The evangelical is unhappy about the terms of the discussion. He feels the definitions of and distinctions in the fact of sin are inadequate. The traditional watchwords are 'deprivation', meaning that the effect of original sin is to deprive mankind of the highest good; and 'depravation', by which is understood that man's original, natural bias towards the higher things has been twisted. The result is that 'we inherit a nature that is not indeed entirely corrupt but which yet has a positive inclination towards evil'.[57] The Church of England, in its Thirty-nine Articles, follows St Augustine and (to some extent at least) John Calvin over against the Council of Trent in holding that human nature is depraved from the course the creator meant it to follow by 'original or birth-sin', that bias 'which draws us to act against the will of God known to us in our conscience'.[58] Anglicans of the evangelical tradition have opposed liberal or anglo-catholic tendencies to soften the 'depravation' teaching.

That fact suggests that evangelicals should see more clearly than catholics or liberals the importance of Mary's freedom from original sin; assuming, that is, that such exemption is theologically desirable and that it does not detract from the fullness of the humanity her Son was to take from her. We must leave over the general consideration of the congruity or otherwise of the Immaculate Conception doctrine with the proportions of the Catholic faith as a whole until we may return to it with the benefit of insights from the other approach to the problem of how to speak of Christ's person; for all our discussion of this theme so far has been in terms of the 'transcendental' approach to the phenomenon of Christ; and, as we have seen, the 'emergent' approach provides a valuable supplement.

We should think then, of God at work in His world from the beginning, the creative Word and the Creator Spirit holding it all in being, within it the surging force of its many processes, gradually leading the potential towards the actual; leaving the choices wherever and at whatever level they were applicable, fostering without dominating; God thoroughly involved in it all, yet exclusively so as to be imprisoned in it, for He remains transcendent as well as involved: the same God who is at work in other forms elsewhere in the universe, the God without whom there can be nothing. We should think of the climax that can be expressed only mythically, where God's image became apparent in a creature capable of responding with acceptance or rejection, capable of moral choice. We should remember the long dreary centuries of frustrated hope which followed the making in all moral seriousness of the wrong choice, with the flawing of human nature which followed. But still as level followed level in advancing human culture and each newly discovered good was turned to disappointing use, the same God was still at work within it all, his traces discernible to the seeing eye in a myriad different ways. But in the twists and turns of pre-history and of history there was one privileged race, one tradition, one milieu in which He made Himself known with particular clarity. The nation in question was outwardly much like any of its contemporaries, and far from the most outstanding. In its own national life, too, there was often little to mark it off from other, less privileged, nations. Yet for all its infidelities there was a line of obedience that never became extinct, however muted its voice. In that thin line that spanned the generations the energies of God were surging towards an unparalleled moment.

And then, 'When the time had fully come, God sent forth his Son, born of a woman, born under the law, to redeem those who were under the law, so that we might receive adoption as sons. And because you are sons, God has sent the Spirit of his Son into our hearts, crying Abba, Father.'[59] 'He came to his own home and his own people received him not. But to all who received him, who believed in his name, he gave power to become children of God.... And the Word became flesh and dwelt among us, full of grace and truth....'[60] St Paul describes in transcendent terms the same climactic event which St John describes in the language of emergence.

The aspect of emergence, as we remarked earlier, requires that the most serious attention be paid to the circumstances in which the Word emerged into human existence with such completeness that He could be described as 'becoming flesh'. His humanity, the long controversies of the early Christian Church made plain, was complete even though there was that disjunction in his parentage which we call the Virgin Birth; and since his humanity was complete, we may use the techniques devised to explore and understand the workings of human nature, though with the proviso that His unlike ours was human nature as it is supposed to be. A like conviction formed the background to a celebrated passage which H. A. Williams included in his contribution to the volume *Soundings*, a symposium of exploratory essays published by Anglican theologians of the University of Cambridge in 1962. The essay was given a devastating critique in a book-length review of the whole volume by Dr Mascall, who was particularly scathing over the reversal of priorities which he detected in the whole essay.[61]

... Freud would certainly not have believed in the Immaculate Conception of Our Lady. But he did show us that a man fully and perfectly developed would have to have had a perfect mother. For Freud no such man had ever existed. Christians have always believed that Our Lord went through a normal human development, and that in him manhood came to its full and perfect expression. The Roman Church, in declaring Our Lady to have been born without taint of original sin, gave expression in a theological idiom to what Freud later discovered in the consulting-room—the overwhelming influence for good or bad which a mother has upon her infant and child.[62]

Dr Mascall may consider the last sentence 'extraordinarily banal', but the point made is well worth making.

The real difficulty with this argument seems to be that it implies, or could imply, an infinite regression: to produce a perfect child requires a perfect mother, who in her turn must have had a perfect mother, and so on. The problem vanishes if we take seriously the interplay in God's activity between the transcendent and the emergent. I have already quoted Dr Taylor's remark about Jesus in whom the Creator Spirit is focused entirely into one human spirit;[63] manhood completely surrendered to, and possessed by, the Spirit of God. 'This is the new kind of man,' Dr Taylor wrote, '... the next unimaginable step forward which man had to take in obedience to the lure of the unfulfilled. But inasmuch as man never could or never would take that step, the God who always works from inside the processes took the step for him, as a man.' Professor Macquarrie reached the same point from the other side when he expressed the traditional transcendent doctrine of Incarnation in terms of the union of a being with Being[64] and found the Virgin Birth to be the appropriate symbol.

If, as we surely must, we take account of the psychological factors involved in the formation of a genuinely human personality, we may accept Father Williams's point, setting it firmly within a theological control which will avoid the danger of infinite regress. To assert that '... the Blessed Virgin Mary, at the first instant of her conception ... was preserved free from all stain of original sin....' allows her to be the point through which the 'New Man' literally emerged, the last link in the long chain of preparation. The doctrine of her Immaculate Conception also enables us to speak of her perfection, so necessary to the awesome demands of her particular motherhood, without detaching that perfection from the grace that came by her Son.

Protestants and Eastern Orthodox may dislike the way in which the Immaculate Conception was proclaimed as a dogma, and the language in which it is framed.[65] But it is capable of being understood in a way which helps us to understand more fully the mystery of Christ, human and divine. It underlines the uniqueness of

73

Mary's vocation to be the mother of God and at the same time her solidarity with sinful mankind who are redeemed by the blood of her Son. Evangelicals may therefore see in the doctrine a valuable if secondary element in the faith of the gospel; and they may work ecumenically towards its elucidation rather than its elimination. They may with a good conscience join with their Catholic and Orthodox brethren in giving thanks for her who, though she was a sinner who rejoiced in her Saviour, was yet able to make the momentous decision on which depended the birth of that Saviour.

IV

Mary the disciple must be seen clearly as one of her Son's people. Anything special in her position derives from that which was special in the Son she bore, and not from her own intrinsic excellence. Any teaching about her which would suggest that she was superior to other people by not requiring the salvation which God brought to the world through her Son must be regarded with the gravest suspicion. If therefore a doctrine, for example that of her Immaculate Conception, were held to show her exemption from the human need for divine grace, it would have to be rejected. But in fact that doctrine may be understood in terms, not of Mary's excellence which in some way led to her salvation, but of the working of divine grace which was accorded her in advance so as to make it possible for the Son of God to take from her His authentic and complete humanity.

The Immaculate Conception of Mary gives the clue to understanding her particular place among her Son's people. She is the first Christian; the first of the redeemed; the first of our flawed human race to have received the fullness of redemption. From first to last—in Catholic dogma, from Immaculate Conception to Assumption—she was a human being transformed by the grace of God into what in the divine purpose she was intended to be. We will therefore now attempt a 'theological life of the Virgin Mary' which will show her to be the prototype of the Christian individual (are far as that term may properly be carried) and of the Christian Church.

Seen in this perspective, the few explicit references in Scripture between them provide a clear profile. Mary's presence in Nazareth at the right moment was no matter of chance; it was part of an operation that originated in the deep centre of God's purposes. The moment was so timed that the circumstances were exactly right; it is interesting to compare St Paul's 'when the time had fully come' in its biblical context of law and the Spirit with St Matthew's account of the wise men from the East who had travelled to worship the king whose birth-star they had seen. The Event which came through Mary was revealed to be in the plan of God by heathen religion as well as in 'what the Lord had spoken by the prophet'.[66] The angel arrived to inaugurate an event for which there had been an immense course of preparation, so that when he told Mary what God had in store for her, she was able to respond to it.[67] It was not, however, her own achievements of human perfection which made her acceptable to God as the mother of His Son, but her readiness to accept God as her Saviour;[68] the implicit humility was the foundation of her obedience.

The theological life of Mary is therefore that of one who was enabled by God's grace to do that which she had been chosen for. The Spirit who overshadowed her for the conception of her Son was no temporary visitor. She was no stranger to his working in the ordinary transformations of grace when he came in that extraordinary manner, and her subsequent recorded actions show that his influence within her remained. The power of redemption was already at work in the one who had borne and brought up the Redeemer. Thus it was that the sufferings which were her lot[69] were the reverse side of her joy in salvation.[70] She was one who heard the Word of God and did it.[71] Most significant is St Luke's last reference to her, when after her Son's Ascension she waited among the disciples in the upper room, praying until the Spirit should come to overshadow the disciples with power and so transform them into the Church which should bear the gospel of her Son into all the world.[72] There can be no doubt over Mary's secure place among her Son's people.

But does she have a special place among them? There are levels at which all who have reflected upon the facts would agree that she has. In the purely historical matter of having been the mother of the incarnate Lord, for example; that could not be repeated, however much of an analogy there may be to it from the formation of Christ in the Christian community.[73] Most people would agree that

Mary's influence continues in that she is an example for the Christian, for the Church. Many devotional homilies on this theme must have been delivered; the pamphlet by the Maréchale earlier quoted was a particularly good example.

At a more profound theological level, the tendency in recent years for theologians of all traditions to return to the earlier sources of Christianity and reappraise, for example, the typology to be found in the writings of the Fathers and in the liturgical texts, has given a new interest to Mary's part as the embodiment or the epitome of the Church in her total obedience to God. An outstanding exposition from a Protestant theologian is *Mary, Mother of the Lord and Figure of the Church* by Max Thurian of the Taizé Community in France.[74] The book ends with a discussion of the vision in the twelfth chapter of the Revelation to St John the Divine, whose interpretation is so important in seeing whether the double symbolism, Mary:Church, goes back to New Testament times. Currently a topic of technical discussion, that is a field where the present writer can make no useful comment.

The title under which Frère Thurian chose to write is strikingly similar, in its precision and its matter, to the title which the Vatican Fathers chose two years later for the very carefully worded[75] eighth chapter of the *Constitution on the Church*: 'The Blessed Virgin Mary, Mother of God, in the Mystery of Christ and the Church'. There is much in common, too, in the conclusions which at many points the two documents draw. But of course there are differences. In length, obviously; for the Vatican document is a mere chapter while Thurian's book is a full-length study. The Vatican Fathers allude in passing to matters which the Protestant monk takes pages to establish. But more importantly, the basic orientation differs between the two treatments. Thurian's central concern is maternity; the parallel between the maternity of Mary and that of the Church. 'Everything that Mary was and has experienced, the Church is and should experience, except for what is bound up with Mary's unique vocation in the incarnation of the Son of God.'[76] He works out this theme in a series of theological studies of the incidents where Mary figures, setting the New Testament accounts in the context of Old Testament fulfilment. Not all his interpretations will command assent, but his book remains a rich source of enlightenment and stimulation even where the reader may perhaps disagree with some detail.

The Vatican chapter has introduced a new note into the discussion which, despite the Roman dogmatic positions which are very naturally taken as accepted, makes it easier to consider the whole matter of Mary from an ecumenical standpoint. Not only is the biblical control to be welcomed[77] but also the biblical perspective which runs through the whole *Constitution on the Church*. Mary appears not simply as the pattern of the Church; but as the pattern of the Church on the move, the Church in its pilgrimage as the wandering people of God. This does not simply mean that the Church is a dynamic body without permanent citizenship in this world.[78] That would be true enough, and important, whether it is interpreted traditionally as referring to the life of the world to come, or in the modern, more secular, this-worldly style. But the Vatican perspective on the Church as God's wandering people is invested with a deeply biblical duality. The Church is on a journey, it is in process of becoming; but at the same time it mysteriously possesses the end to which it is journeying, it is what it is becoming; and also, it is the sign of the end to which it is journeying.

The emphasis, as we have said, runs through the whole *Constitution* and is one of the chief factors which make that document so encouraging a text for ecumenical discussion. It moves (despite differences of vocabulary) in a world of discourse which has evident points of contact with the missiological writing of Dr John Taylor; it reminds one, too, of Dr Flanagan's plea for deeper appreciation of the workings of the Spirit, a point to which we shall return later. For the present, we should notice the place accorded in the Vatican's perspective to the Church as the pilgrim people to the Virgin. We may cite the last paragraph but one, in the translation edited by Mgr Gallagher:[79]

In the bodily and spiritual glory which she possesses in heaven, the Mother of Jesus continues in this present world as the image and the first flowering of the Church as she is to be perfected in the world to come. Likewise Mary shines forth on earth, until the day that the Lord shall come (cf. 2 Pet.3.10), as a sign of sure hope and solace for the pilgrim People of God.

The language here is of course coloured by acceptance of the dogma of Mary's bodily Assumption. We shall consider that teaching partly later in this chapter and partly in the next. But the message of the Council says something of great importance even without such dogmatic reinforcement. It shows that Mary is not merely an example for the Church to follow; it is not just that she sums up in herself all that the Church ought to be, and ultimately will be. Those are no doubt consequences, but so long as we are thinking in moralistic terms we shall miss the real point; one which is understood well by the Eastern Orthodox Church who do not accept the Western dogma; one from failure to accept which Protestant Christianity is sadly weakened. Mary is the one who has, so to speak, got there. She is the human being, wholly one with all other human beings, entirely created, entirely supported by divine grace, from first to last yielded to the Holy Spirit—whose response has been total and who therefore stands in the final state of human fulfilment.

One of the tasks of the next chapter will be the attempt to be more specific about human fulfilment. For the moment we may take two of the many New Testament images which bear upon it. The first should perhaps be called an anti-image; it is St John's great 'Beloved, we are God's children now; it does not yet appear what we shall be, but we know that when he appears we shall be like him, for we shall see him as he is. . . .'[80] The other passage is St Paul's towering affirmation of faith: 'We know that in everything God works for good with those who love him, who are called according to his purpose. For those whom he foreknew he also predestined to be conformed to the image of his Son, in order that he might be the first-born among many brethren. And those whom he predestined he also called; and those whom he called he also justified; and those whom he justified he also glorified.'[81]

I believe that just as we may see in the theological life of the Virgin Mary, as the Scriptures describe her, a model of justification by faith, so we may view the beginning and the end of her story which later traditions, held in different ways by Eastern Orthodox and Roman Catholic, have added on to the scriptural deposit, not as distortion from it but as congruent with it and so as legitimate extensions. It is of course possible to hold these doctrines and to express them in such a way that they do effectively do violence to the integrity of the received faith and so come under the hammer of

St Paul's anathema called down on those who preach 'another gospel'.[82] But I cannot see why in themselves they should be thus expressed. It seems to me that they fall more naturally under the theological control of the great evangelical centralities of the faith. I have earlier expounded Mary's Immaculate Conception in terms of that control.[83] Surely it is equally possible to think of her Assumption as the end of the great Pauline series; Mary the woman whose predestination has been advanced to its full term of conformation into the image of God's son and hers; Mary who was called and who responded totally; Mary who was justified and rejoiced in her salvation; Mary who has been glorified? If it may be so taken, and Mary may be seen as the one of us who has already 'got there', then it gives great force to the insistence of the Vatican *Constitution* that Mary is a sign of sure hope and solace for the wandering People of God; and it makes her a splendid trophy of the gospel's grace and power.

Some years ago I had the honour to address one of the first meetings of The Ecumenical Society of the Blessed Virgin Mary.[84] In the course of the paper I advanced the suggestions about interpreting the Assumption which I have just made. But on that occasion I did so much more tentatively. I went on to describe four factors which might make it difficult for Protestants to accept the doctrine even on that interpretation. It is worth looking at these objections again and seeing how much force they have.

The first objection concerned the silence of Scripture. In so far as the Assumption is a dogma to be believed as necessary for salvation, the objection still stands. But that is no reason why, if it is held to be congruent with Scripture, it may not be maintained as a true doctrine.

The second objection concerned the early history of the belief, recounted for example by the Italian Protestant scholar Giovanni Miegge.[85] He points out that accounts of Mary's 'falling asleep' are based on late works of piety and are quite unrelated to the historical traditions of the primitive Church; and these works, which mostly date from the century following the Council of Ephesus with its first formal description of Mary as *Theotokos*, Mother of God,[86] represent a debased, popular Christianity which has made common cause with the many forms of mother-goddess worshipped in Mediterranean lands from the dawn of history. The various pious tales

79

differ widely in detail. Miegge quotes a Catholic scholar, M. Jugie: 'From the historical point of view, their value is absolutely nothing.... From the doctrinal point of view they ... inform us on the first solutions that Christian piety gave to the problems posed by Mary's death.'[87]

It is difficult to disagree with Miegge's assembly of facts concerning the historical origins of the belief. But it is not necessary to accept all his background assumptions; concerning, most notably, the evil conjunction of Christian piety with the primeval mother-goddess. Indeed, a careful reading of the many apocryphal as well as later patristic texts which he quotes suggests that the former as well as the latter were careful not to allow Mary, however glorified, to have stepped over the line which separates human beings from God; and the example which concludes his *catena* of legendary accounts is one which, in his own words, 'is an answer to the need of emphasizing Mary's complete humanity that is complementary to her idealization'. Many of the stories are formally heretical, and many of them are very silly; but they are not concerned with the worship of a goddess.

Miegge describes as a second stage in the evolution of the doctrine the work of very late patristic theologians, notably Andrew of Crete (660–740) and John of Damascus (died 749) among the Easterns. These writers, who summarize the developed early Eastern tradition, base their teaching on Mary's Assumption into heaven not on history, but on 'necessity', 'becomingness'. 'It is interesting,' Miegge writes, 'to note that the doctrine of the Assumption has, in these its first authoritative representatives, the same character of theological construction of suitability and analogy which today are seen again in the more developed and modern representations.'[88] Miegge's 'today' was, of course, the exuberant years of Pope Pius XII when Mariology flourished as a theological discipline in its own right; the Dogma of the Assumption was proclaimed in the same year that Professor Miegge published the original Italian edition of his book. But his point still stands; and even if, as I have suggested, evangelicals may with integrity accept the teaching as theologically valid, they will still resist its imposition upon the faithful as necessary to be believed for salvation.

Before leaving the second possible objection, a word should be said about the late hour at which the doctrine appeared. Mariology is essentially secondary. It is, as became apparent earlier, only when the person of Christ, human and divine, has become clear and has been made the subject of reflection, that the person of his mother comes to the fore. We shall see in the next chapter that Mary's place among her Son's disciples and the consequent efficacy of her prayers impressed the Christian mind earlier than did the problems posed by the physical corruption of the human body from which the Saviour took his flesh. The fact that teaching about the Lord's mother did not begin to receive doctrinal attention until after she had, on account of her Son, become known as *Theotokos*, in no way invalidates that attention; the contrary is rather true.

The third objection was that all teaching about Mary which concerned her rather than her Son was unnecessary. Jesus himself was 'the first-born among many brethren' (clearly the meaning of the phrase in the passage from the Epistle to the Romans which I cited). It sometimes seems that the emphasis on his mother in the Catholic and Orthodox traditions reflects doubt upon the genuineness of his humanity. It was this objection, so characteristic of contemporary thought about Christ, which led to the long exposition of the 'brotherness' and the 'otherness' of Jesus in the preceding chapter. There is nothing which may be usefully added at this point. The reader who wishes to ponder the matter further may refer to chapter 2, sections III to V.

The fourth objection was the familiar evangelical protestant one that Mariological doctrines emasculate the strong biblical emphasis on divine grace, supplementing the saving activity of God by a wholly improper intrusion of human merit. Again, this matter has already been treated: in sections II to VIII of this present chapter. We may simply add the text from the Epistle to the Ephesians with which the evangelical Anglican Philip Hughes ends his opening chapter which describes 'what grace is': 'By grace have you been saved through faith; and this is not your own doing, it is the gift of God: not because of works, lest any man should boast.'[89] No text could better illustrate the true position of the Blessed Virgin Mary among her Son's people.

4

Mary, Mother of Her Son's People

I

Christians, both as individuals and in their groupings, differ greatly in their understanding of Mary as mother; that is, how far her motherhood extends. Those who belong to Churches which make much of her, Orthodox and Catholics, tend to regard her as their own spiritual mother and to involve her in their own religious lives at various sensitive points. Those for whom she is confined to the pages of history do not, and are scandalized at what they regard as her intrusion into a region properly reserved for God alone. The present chapter is therefore bound to deal with matters which arouse emotions; the heart can rule the head so vigorously that arguments are ignored. A writer on the theme, particularly one who attempts a mediating position, must note carefully the main emotional points.

There is obviously a special quality in Mary's motherhood. We considered at length the different levels in the relationship with her Son, which set her apart from all other mothers as well as giving her kinship with them. Primarily she was the mother of Jesus—that is, it was from her body that he drew his human flesh, and for nine months she carried him about in her womb. It is evident that, since the incarnation was no temporary episode in the life of the Son of God but the permanent assuming of human nature, the relationship established by his birth was one which endured. Equally obviously, it was one which changed. Every mother-and-son relationship must change unless it is to become distorted. The relationship of Mary and her Son changed more than others; for the boy became not merely a man, but a man who was the Lord, the Word made flesh, the Son of God. It is unprofitable and perhaps impious to try to speculate on the feelings of the mother of Jesus as she learned what it meant to be the mother of God.

Something, however, has to be said, unless the vital matter of her motherhood is to go by default. It is better said, perhaps, by the poet or the artist than by the theologian who has to keep to the syntax of ordinary discourse. There is a peculiarly unattractive type of banality which afflicts the theologian when he attempts to express his filial devotion to Mary; too often an aesthetic offence is added to the theological obstacle which confronts the would-be sympathetic Protestant inquirer. There are honourable exceptions; of Catholic works which appeared before the Second Vatican Council, special mention should be made of Jean Guitton's *The Blessed Virgin*.[1] The dedication of his book, 'To M. l'Abbé Vernhet and to our Protestant, Anglican, and Orthodox brethren, that the Virgin of Cana may hasten the hour of union' is of obvious importance to those who have followed the argument of this book so far; his appreciation of the relevance of the Blessed Virgin to the Protestant insistence on the absolute sovereignty of grace and justification by faith alone gives the book a new importance in the post-conciliar days;[2] and we shall refer later to the attributes which he would like to see paid to the Virgin in future devotion.[3] And among English works we should emphasize the anthology edited in the austere post-war years by Elizabeth Rothenstein, *The Virgin and the Child*. It is a profoundly evocative volume which brings together great paintings or their details (unfortunately not in colour) with English verse which is perceptive theologically as well as poetically.[4]

It is Jean Guitton who makes the point most clearly:

The art most appropriate to the Blessed Virgin is the painter's. By a sure instinct this aesthetic relation was grasped at the outset: hence the tradition that St Luke painted a portrait of the Virgin. Sculpture cannot render what is so important in a woman, vivacity of expression. But the sculptor has one advantage over the painter: from a single block of stone he can draw forth a group—a Mother and Child. And the smooth curves of ivory made a perfect medium for the promise and innocent hope of childhood. Perhaps surprisingly, architecture seems to be the art most powerfully inspired by the Blessed Virgin. Already in pagan times the Parthenon had been dedicated to the virgin Athene. After the sixth century it was turned into a Christian church of the *Theotokos*; as if purity were best translated by mere proportion.[5]

Perhaps surprisingly, it is an art historian of uncompromisingly Protestant convictions, Professor H. R. Rookmaaker of the Free University of Amsterdam, who shows how pictorial art can make clear as words cannot the several strands which go to make up the unique motherhood of Mary. He is commenting on a Duccio *Madonna with Child* to be seen in the Museo dell' Opera del Duomo at Siena. He expounds the picture in a chapter headed 'The message in the medium'. Duccio's picture 'tells us obviously about the Madonna, called the Mother of God—that alone would be good enough reason to depict Christ as a baby. The Madonna is looking at us, and seems interested in us, even if in rather an aloof way. She obviously is no ordinary person—not even the greatest blasphemer could make a pin-up girl out of her, nor would she make an advertisement for child care. She is more than human, yet still human. This is what the picture tells us. It is a sermon on Mary, if you like. In a deep and truly religious sense, the picture was a "poster" telling people to go to Mary with all their troubles.'[6]

Duccio, as is well known,[7] stood with Cimabue of Florence and Cavallini of Rome at the very dawn of those Italian traditions of painting which led to the Renaissance; he was of the generation before Cimabue's great pupil Giotto. The Duccio painting reproduced in Rookmaaker's book stands in obvious relation to Orthodox iconography, first Greek and then (contemporary with Western developments), Russian.[8] An Eastern Orthodox theologian like the Russian *émigré* Nicolas Zernov might find Duccio deficient in his understanding of Orthodox representational symbolism at a particular point,[9] but in his grasp of Mary's significance as a mother of a human baby who was also the Word of God incarnate, Duccio is a reliable theological painter of icons; if his painting is not that of the almost legendary eleventh-century *Our Lady of Vladimir*, it is nearer to it in time and not much further from it in spirit than Andrew Rublev's seminal early fifteenth-century copy.[10]

No doubt it would be expecting too much to hope to find the painting of the Lord's mother which tradition ascribes to the time of St Luke. We are, however, on safe ground in going back a long way further than Rublev or his Russian prototype. 'In the years that follow' the Council of Ephesus, 431, which declared Mary to be *Theotokos*, '... she is seen in Rome as a queen, domina....

Yet her definitive portrait emerges from the East, perhaps from Palestine or from Constantinople. There she is a tranquil, mature figure, wrapped from head to foot in a dark blue mantle and veil. ... She is always shown in one of three positions: standing ...; frontally enthroned with her child upon her knee ...; or else alone, standing in an attitude of prayer, with outstretched arms, a symbol of the Church, ever persevering in prayer. This last image is first found in pictures of the Ascension ..., where she clearly prepresents the Church left behind, persisting in faith and prayer, amid the troubled apostles (cf. Acts 1.14)....'[11]

The picture of the Ascension with Mary standing in the midst of the bewildered disciples shows us the earliest and the most basic notion of Mary as mother of her Son's people. It is an image to be found as early as 580 to 600, the date given to a small wooden reliquary with souvenirs from Palestine. The design is one of five panels which decorate the lid. The figures, as in so much early Christian painting, seem crude. Their design is important. 'It is thought', write the authors of *Atlas of the Early Christian World*, 'that the five tableaux reflect the Palestinian iconography (perhaps the mosaics at the Holy Places themselves?).'[12] The picture of the Ascension is already 'the classical Byzantine composition' which suggests a very early date indeed for it to have first become a focus for Christian pictorial reflection.

An interesting feature is that although this icon of the Ascension is closely based upon St Luke's description in the first chapter of the Acts, it is not an illustration of it. St Luke relates two separate incidents, distinguished in time and in place. The Ascension took place apparently on 'the mount called Olivet', the hills to the east of Jerusalem across the Kidron valley (problems caused by St Luke's other, briefer account at the end of his Gospel do not concern the present discussion). The implication is that the only people present were 'the apostles whom he had chosen', and events at the end of the chapter show that that phrase must be strictly interpreted to mean the Twelve less the traitor Judas. The witnesses to the Ascension then went back to Jerusalem, 'a sabbath day's journey away'. It was in the upper room there that the Eleven, 'together with the women and Mary the mother of Jesus, and with his brothers ... with one accord devoted themselves to prayer'. It seems therefore that the primitive iconography has fused together the two scriptural incidents.

I do not believe that this fusion is either accidental or due to carelessness. I believe rather that it represents a doctrinal development which is both legitimate and profound, bringing the Lucan tradition into relation with the Johannine and so indicating the line of development for a biblically controlled Mariology. It is a theological development expressed in terms of pictorial representation; and it is therefore appropriate to discuss it in iconographical terms before turning to the account in systematic theology.

Manolis Chatzidakis, Ephor General of Antiquities at Athens, in his concise and informative introduction to the icons in the Byzantine Museum there, traces the origins of icon painting to the funerary portraits of Hellenistic Egypt.[13] Nicolas Zernov makes the same point; 'The persons commemorated in these striking pictures wanted to be remembered by the living when they left this familiar world for an unknown and disembodied existence.... Accordingly, the departed was represented in the prime of life, young, handsome, attractive, with large, wide-open eyes, the intention being so to impress the minds of the living with his bodily form as to escape (at least partially) the total oblivion of death.'[14] Dr Zernov traces an unbroken tradition, complete with such continuing conventions as eyes which look straight into those of the beholder, from the hot African desert to the marshy damp of the Russian north sixteen centuries later. The inner core which maintains intact the whole tradition is 'the underlying conviction that men have found in art an effective weapon in their struggle against total annihilation.'[15]

Dr Zernov stresses that the icon tradition runs from pagan times into Christian. The tradition is unbroken, but its course is modified by the crisis of conversion. Similar staring eyes peer out from the pagan and the Christian faces, making and maintaining contact strong enough to breach the barrier of death. But there is an enormous difference. The eyes in the Christian icon were, to quote Dr Zernov, 'no longer the anxious eyes of a person looking with longing on the world dear to him which he was reluctant to leave. On the contrary, the eyes of the saints testify to the peace and contentment of one who has reached his Father's home. The saints called Christians to follow in their footsteps.... They wanted also to be remembered, but with a different purpose in view.'[16] There were other differences between the pagan and the Christian icons, differences which are theological as well as stylistic. 'For example,' Dr Zernov writes, 'the shape of the face was altered. Sensual exuberance was discarded by making the mouth smaller, and the nose thinner and longer.'[17] It is an error to confuse the overcoming of the flesh with contempt for it. Again, it is the eyes which establish the true meaning. 'Eastern Christians', declares Dr Zernov, 'do not despise the body. Even less do they regard it as an obstacle to communion with the divine, but they believe it needs purification and regeneration, and the icons are a confirmation of this belief. This victory over the flesh is expressed through the eyes which reflect the eternal bliss experienced by those who have established harmony with their Creator.'[18] We have met this emphasis in the exchange of eye with eye earlier in the book; in Dr Taylor's analysis of a painting of the Annunciation belonging to a very different artistic and theological tradition, that of the Italian Renaissance.[19]

An icon is thus not merely a religious painting; it is a focus of spiritual meeting. It is not necessary for our purposes to go deeply into the Orthodox theology of icons. It is enough to establish with Dr Chatzidakis that 'the likeness of the figure to the holy person it represents, is an indispensable factor by which the icon justified its role as an intermediary between the spiritual and terrestrial worlds, and by which the divine grace belonging to the sacred person should be transmitted to the icon. According to a semi-official definition, "the icon is a simulacrum which reproduces the characteristics of the subject but with certain differences". From this conception the character of the portrait is derived and, by extension, the authenticity of depicted scenes proceeds.'[20] The stylization and the degree of abstraction to be found in icons are thus basically matters of theological rather than aesthetic convention.

Dr Zernov throws light upon the theology behind the conventions in what he has to say about icons which show whole scenes. 'Those depicting passages from the Gospels stress the approach of the New Testament that is so powerfully expressed in Orthodox worship, namely that the life of the Incarnate Lord breaks through the barrier of time and takes place in an eternal present. . . . This present does not make history less important; on the contrary, the

Orthodox Church can use the word "today"—(for example, "Today He has risen from the dead")—with such confidence because it believes that all the great and decisive events of the Gospel are historical facts, and that there was a day when each event took place; but their significance is such that their effects are still operative.'

'The other aspect of Orthodox worship,' Dr Zernov goes on, 'the viewing of history in the light of its theological and mystical implications, also finds full expression in the icons. Their masters are never satisfied with mere factual account but add theological commentaries.'[21] Such a statement must be read against the background of tradition maintained with great loyalty; in Western painting (or Western theology) it would suggest a degree of innovation or personal preference quite foreign to the Eastern way. Dr Chatzidakis clarifies the difference between tradition and mere copying by observing the differences which exist between the newly created work and the prototype. His analysis centres on a certain withdrawal from the material aspect of the subject; a measure of abstraction. But it is a withdrawal conditioned by principles of a stylistic order '... founded upon spiritual laws which were stimulated by a profound, often ardent, faith. The knowledge of these aesthetic and spiritual laws and the knowledge of the spiritual mission of a work of art were universally accepted as part of the natural religious function. These are the factors which, in the art of icon painting, create a transubstantiation of beings and things into forms which are both comprehensible in the world we inhabit and different from it. Thus, this likeness and non-likeness constitute a dialectical antimony, inherent in Byzantine painting, which confers a spiritual value that penetrates the art and creates a means of mystical intercession between the intelligible and the sensible world.'[22]

I have stressed the interplay of theological and stylistic factors in the Eastern Orthodox understanding of the icons which are so characteristic a feature of its Christian life, because there seems to be at least an analogy between that process and the doctrinal development of Christian reflection upon the basic deposit of faith. To observe the analogy may protect the pragmatic Western theological mind from isolating the intellectual element in the theological process. But there may be also a further reason for taking seriously the iconographic process, a closer parallel than that of analogy. It could be that the artist and the theologian working within the life of the Church in its pilgrimage through history are making their own distinct but mutually complementary response to the Holy Spirit guiding them into the fullness of truth. It is on that Johannine assumption[23] that we return to the early icon of the Lord's mother among the disciples at her Son's Ascension.

II

The unknown artist who first went beyond the letter of Scripture by painting Mary in his icon of the Ascension was, whether or not he knew it, expressing a profound and permanent element in the true nature of the Church of which he was part. The composition as it is reproduced in the *Atlas of the Early Christian World*[24] is strong and clear. The panel is slightly longer than it is high and it is divided into an upper and a lower half. In the upper half, the seated figure of Christ, his hand raised in blessing, is ascending in an oval shape, presumably a stylized cloud, while flying angels on either side support the vehicle in an almost heraldic manner. There is a clear sense of rising. On the ground twelve figures divided into two groups of six to the left and to the right stand or lean in varying attitudes suggestive of disarray. Between the two groups, and immediately under the majestic figure of her ascending Son, stands the mother in her long blue robe, her hands raised in the liturgical gesture of supplication.

Evidently the presence of Mary is not the only liberty which the artist has taken with the scriptural account. He has included twelve other figures, not eleven; Judas has been replaced. We need not be alarmed; for in the previous chapter the difference was made plain between an icon of an event and an illustration of it for inclusion in the book. What we have here is not merely a pictorial substitute for the biblical account, nor a visual aid for slow readers. It is a statement of what the Ascension means in the continuing life of the Ascended Lord's people. As such, it has been amplified by elements from elsewhere in the Christian tradition. In that sense it may perhaps be considered as a visual counterpart to those many passages in the New Testament epistles where the writers draw out the significances—the many and varied significances—of the return of Jesus to his Father.

We discussed one such abiding significance in the first section of this book, where one of the two principal features in the 'otherness' of Jesus was his strange presence while being physically absent.[25] The blessings of his presence continued in the protection and furtherance of his people after his bodily withdrawal from them. So it is in the icon that the eye is drawn first to the figure of Jesus, ascending; sitting, the posture of ruling and judging; majestic, 'other', attended by angels who are supporting him as slaves;[26] and yet benevolent, friendly even, blessing.[27] He is the *mysterium tremendum* yet he is also *fascinans*. Jesus in the icon is true to the biblical picture, numinous in the proper sense of 'beckoning' amid all his disturbing strangeness.[28]

But his people in the lower half of the picture are in disarray. Initially no doubt the reference is to the Acts account of the Ascension, where the surviving Eleven were in double disarray: because of their natural bewilderment at their master's strange disappearance, with its Old Testament overtones of Jehovah's dangerous and awful presence; but also because of their crass inability to discern their departing master's purposes, shown by their inquiry at such a moment for a timetable of the divine plan.[29] But the inclusion of the twelfth figure prevents us from taking the disarray to be merely that of the particular occasion. It is the disarray which haunts the Church in its more sensitive moments, the hopelessness which so often afflicts Christians in what appears to be a world that God has forsaken. The disarray of the apostles is a piece of realism.

But it is not the whole of realism. That, too, is made clear in the icon. The apostles, according to the Acts, returned to Jerusalem; and, in company with the women, and Mary the mother of Jesus, and with his brothers, they devoted themselves to prayer. The last words of Jesus had been a promise that the Spirit of power would come upon the apostles, thus enabling them to be witnesses to Jesus throughout the world. The promise was fulfilled and the prayers were answered, of course, on the day of Pentecost. The Church emerged from the uncertain twilight and simultaneously its mission began.

The icon shows Mary in prayer beneath the ascending Lord while the disciples—twelve, not eleven—are still suffering from shock.

Her presence between the two groups of apostles, recollected and engaged on the proper business which they were not, suggests that she is not merely an individual but a representative figure, 'Mother Church' as well as the mother of the Church's Lord; perhaps also the mother in the Church; perhaps also the 'mother' of the Church's members. Before we investigate these distinctions, however, it will be well to look at another theological dimension suggested by the icon of the Ascension.

The icon includes elements which suggest an influence from St John's Gospel, and that may lie behind the modifications which the artist has made in St Luke's account. One element is the apparently straightforward one of Mary's position among the disciples; the other element concerns the way events are understood within the sequence of time. The second element underlies the first and will be dealt with accordingly.

St Luke gave close attention to precise statements of time. It was his exact dating of the birth of Jesus, placing it in relation to personalities and events in the great world, which chiefly earned him his reputation as the 'historian' among the gospel-writers.[30] A conviction that chronological sequence is important dominates the way in which he organizes the material for his account of the Christian mission and its origins. It is to St Luke that we owe the tradition of the 'great forty days' which separated the Resurrection of Jesus from his Ascension.[31] He is less specific over the interval between the Ascension and the coming of the Spirit, though the clear implication is that it was (as the subsequent Calendar of the Church made it) a period of ten days. 'The day of Pentecost was so called because it was celebrated on the fiftieth (GK *pentekoste*) day after the presentation of the first harvested sheaf of the barley harvest, i.e. the fiftieth day from the first Sunday after Passover.'[32] More recent studies of St Luke have abandoned the notion that he was an historian to the exclusion of all but minimal theological concerns;[33] it remains clear that the intervals of time play a big part in his theological understanding. The events which heralded the new age of fulfilment by the Spirit followed one another in an orderly sequence.

It is otherwise according to St John. We discussed earlier[34] the concentration upon the 'hour' of Jesus, which arrived when Jesus engaged in decisive victorious combat with the powers of evil. We spoke then in terms of death and resurrection. Those events were the heart of the combat, but the total 'event' of Jesus, according to St John's perspective, is more complex. It is death-resurrection-ascension-sending of the Spirit, a unity of life-giving action whose strands cannot be wholly unpicked; like the tunic of Jesus for which the execution squad cast lots, it is all one piece.

The hints of the total action which glitter like occasional jewels in the action of the first twelve chapters of the Gospel are focused into explanation in the talks with the disciples which run from the thirteenth chapter to the climax of the great prayer in the seventeenth. The explanations, however, were not to be understood at once. They look forward to the events which were about to unroll: events of a few days described in the eighteenth, nineteenth, and twentieth chapters, but whose effects, according to the twenty-first chapter (which may have been added later by another hand), remain until the Lord's return.

The events which St Luke sets down so carefully in order all figure in St John in one way or another, but not in order. There is no account of the Ascension—a matter to be considered shortly—but on the morning of the Resurrection Jesus told Mary Magdalene not to touch him: 'For I have not yet ascended to the Father; but go to my brethren and say to them, I am ascending to my Father and your Father, to my God and your God.' On the same day—Easter day—he appeared to the disciples and, having shown them his wounds by way of credentials, said to them: 'Peace be with you. As the Father has sent me, even so I send you.' 'And', the evangelist adds, 'when he had said this, he breathed on them, and said to them, "Receive the Holy Spirit. If you forgive the sins of any, they are forgiven; if you retain the sins of any, they are retained."'[35] If we compare that sequence with St Luke's, we see that the fifty days have been reduced to one and the giving of the Spirit comes before the (undescribed) Ascension.

Which account is right? But then, what does 'right' mean in such a context? I believe that St Luke is right historically. He was at such pains to get the most accurate traditions current when he wrote[36] that it seems unlikely that he was misled in such a matter. Also, his order seems right psychologically. The events had been of such a disturbing nature that the apostles must have needed time to adjust to them. For similar reasons the institutional Church has been rightly guided in accepting St Luke's sequence as the basis of its Christian year. The human mind cannot understand the truth without some measure of mediation. St Luke follows events accurately, recording how they were teased out on the comb of passing time. A sight of the separate strands helps towards the appreciation of the whole fabric.

But it carries its dangers. The truth is one and indivisible. It is the work of God, who stands outside time, for time only exists because He wills it. St John's order of events bears witness to the unity, the simultaneity, of God's action. Perhaps that is why he gives no account of the Ascension, even though Jesus in the fourth Gospel speaks so much more about 'returning to his Father' than he does in the other three. Words so easily give an impression not intended. The later twentieth century, so deeply marked by technology, by the exploration of space, finds it hard to understand the traditional language of Ascension. The Lucan sequence too easily suggests the myth of a God who arrived from outer space, took up temporary residence on earth, and then went back to his own place. The Johannine sequence provides a corrective by looking at the same events from a different vantage point. Jesus really did go out from God and return to Him, yet whoever really saw him had also seen the Father.[37] He was not yet an old man and yet he was older than Abraham.[38] He was the resurrection and the life even though in the order of time he had yet to die.[39] He did ascend to the Father, but his absence was not to be such as to leave the disciples bereft of his support;[40] the evangelist describes the arrival of that support but not the departure of the one through whom it came.

There is then a wholeness in the meaning which St John gives to the facts about Jesus, a wholeness which demands a certain simultaneity of presentation; and that balances the chronological extension of St Luke's narratives. This wholeness transcending time (though without damage to historical actuality) provides the basic perspective in which to read St John's account of Mary at the foot of the cross:

'Standing by the cross of Jesus were his mother, and his mother's sister, Mary, the wife of Clopas, and Mary Magdalene. When Jesus saw his mother, and the disciple whom he loved standing near, he said to his mother. "Woman, behold your son!" Then he said to the disciple, "Behold your mother!" And from that hour the disciple took her to his own home.'[41]

We considered this passage briefly earlier[42] and found reason to support those commentators who see here a symbolic account of the birth of the Church, born from the cross. We left over for discussion now the further question of whether we should understand from the passage that all disciples should look upon the Lord's mother as their own and expect from her a mother's care; though in fact we shall find it to be not one question but many.

A starting point will be to return to the icon of the Ascension. Mary's presence beneath the ascending Lord, erect and composed in prayer between two groups of dishevelled-looking apostles, suggested that she was not there simply as a private person but as a representative one. She was the Church correctly responding, 'Mother Church'. We can go a stage further in drawing out the significance of that if we take the icon to have modified the original Lucan Ascension scene from the thought of St John. The Mary who stands at the centre of the group is not simply the Mary who appears, as it were, behind the apostles waiting in prayer; she is also the Mary who stood with the other women at the foot of the cross, the Mary whom her Son committed to the disciple whom he loved so as to form not an annexe to, but the nucleus of, the Church that is born from the cross. It is thus the Johannine modification which has brought Mary, albeit beneath her Son, to the centre of the picture.

A further Johannine modification is the scrambling of St Luke's table of time. We have already remarked on the full complement of apostles and the implication that the icon is less an illustration of the Ascension than a statement about the Ascension in the continuing life of the Church. The Ascension was the departure of the Lord from the view of his Church, but it was also a departure to the right hand of power, a departure which was expedient for his people since it meant the releasing among them of the Holy Spirit.[43] Further, the Ascension is the return to the Father not only of the victorious Son of God, the work which his Father had sent him to do completed,[44] but the Word made flesh returning to God. It is thus a most adequate symbol of the new life by which the Church lives, a point of convergence for many of the central Christian convictions.

It seems therefore that the figure of Mary in the icon is primarily that of the representative disciple. As mother of their Lord, she was 'the human being nearest to God' and her presence at the Church's birth in both Lucan and Johannine schemes reinforces the natural conclusion that she was close to him in spirit too. Her place in the icon's grouping seems to show her more as their sister than as their mother, except in the general sense of 'Mother Church'. Likewise her posture suggests the continued prayer of the faithful Church, however unfaithful its individual members might be; it does not of itself imply belief in the particular efficacy of her prayers as an individual. It is of course true that to assert one meaning as primary is not thereby to deny the existence of other meanings.

We must now take leave of the little icon of the Ascension. But before passing on to the next topic a few words should be said about the confusion caused by careless use of family terms. It seems to me beyond serious doubt that St John understands the Church as a family born from the cross, and the nucleus of that family is to be found in the new relationship of mother and son which Jesus established from the cross. It is a fair deduction that all those who are Christ's disciples can claim Mary as their mother. But how far are we to press the metaphor? After all, it is one among many related ways of speaking. If it is taken too literally, it would provoke the question which earned Nicodemus his rebuke: 'How can a man be born when he is old? Can he enter a second time into his mother's womb, and be born?'[45] And how does the thought of Mary as mother relate to the more prominent biblical theme— Johannine as well as Pauline—of our adoption through relationship with Christ as children of God; or to the rebirth taught in the first letter of St Peter?

There are two principal dangers in unguarded speech about these matters. The first is to combine too easily ways of expressing the newness of life which Christ brings. The biblical authors each use the phrases they do within the integrity of their individual thought. It is dangerous to conflate similar turns of phrase which are not identical, in the interest of an overriding theory. The truth may be better served by a splendid riot of metaphor.

There is, too, the particular danger of looking upon Mary as one's mother in such a way as to imply a practical equivalence with the Fatherhood of God. It is sometimes said that the excessive masculinity of God in Christian tradition needs to be modified by a female figure; and that that figure is our Lady. There is certainly an element of truth in the over-masculine development of Christianity. But to erect the mother of Jesus into a divine spouse (other than in the unique incarnation of the Son of God) comes perilously near to making the Trinity into a quaternity; which evil condemns itself.

III

It is impossible to speak more clearly about Mary's maternal functions among her Son's people without further inquiry into the nature of those 'people'. The trouble with the word 'church' is its differing associations. It may be said at once that, theologically, the word is concerned with people, not buildings; and with people gathered into a community rather than with people as a collection of individuals. It is the confusions in the use of the word, and indeed the confusions which Christian divisions and denominations have made in the meaning of it, that have caused us to write in terms of Mary and her Son's people. That term is not as imprecise as it may sound; for whatever definition is chosen to control the notion of the Church, it must include the element of relationship with her Son.

The early Christians did not sit down to define the Church. The experience of discipleship during the life of Jesus carried with it a sense of community; disciples belonged not only to their master, but to each other. At first, all being Jewish disciples of a Jewish teacher, they saw themselves as a particular group within Israel, itself looked upon for centuries as not just a nation or people among the nations or peoples of the world, but as the People of God. Their nation was 'called out' from among the other nations to know God especially well; and 'called out' is the root meaning of *ekklesia*, the basic word for 'church' in the Greek New Testament. Thus the earliest Christians held the loyalties which bound them particularly to their master and to each other within the framework of Israel's traditional loyalties. From the start, however, conflict with the Israelite authorities made it clear that the two loyalties could not be represented by the simple diagram of a small circle within a large one. It was claimed that the new loyalties were the fulfilment of the old ones.

The small beginnings of the Christian Church in the disciples gathered loyally round their teacher has always remained at the heart of Christian corporate self-awareness. It has been subject to enormous modifications, of which four of the most important happened in the period covered by the New Testament documents. A fifth had begun to be important before the New Testament period closed, but because it had not reached anything like the size it has later become, it is not so well documented as the other four.

The first change was the removal of Jesus and the strange discovery that though physically absent he was in some sense present. Loyalty to him remained, but it did not (as might have been supposed) become loyalty to the teachings and memory of a revered though dead master. Further, despite rivalries of various sorts, the loyalty of the disciples to each other deepened. The reality of God which they called Holy Spirit, formed them into a unity with their master and with each other. As their reflection carried them further into understanding what was happening, phrases like 'in Christ', 'members of Christ', 'members of one another' seemed appropriate. There were certain signs and rituals, also, which defined their unity: notably baptism and the shared meal they called 'the breaking of bread' or, because he had told them to do it, 'the Lord's supper'.

The second change was geographical and numerical. The commission the Lord had given the apostles (that word is the English version of the Greek word for 'sent') was, when the Spirit had come, to bear witness to him as the Fulfiller. They did so, with notable effect. The small intimacy of the upper room was replaced by a horde of strangers.... Furthermore, the new disciples did not all stay in Jerusalem—indeed, most of them were pilgrims up from anywhere round the Mediterranean trade routes, and, of course, they went home. The organizational problems were enormous. That they did not prove insuperable depended on two factors. All the new followers of the Way (to use one of their earliest names for themselves) were Jews, and would be members of their local synagogue. There was no necessary breach; followers of the Way could, initially at least, remain as adherents of minority teaching within the synagogue. If, or rather, when, their obedience to the new loyalty led to their expulsion, they could still copy the synagogue's precedent of local groups expressing the life shared by the whole people. The second factor, underlying and influencing the process, and no doubt smoothing out some of the human difficulties, was the Holy Spirit whose work of gathering into one was not confined to one place.

The third modification was the decision to admit Gentiles. How traumatic that was can be seen from the way in which St Peter, who started the practice against all his prejudices, had to defend his actions before his colleagues;[46] and yet later, himself drew back from some of the consequences.[47]

The fourth change resulted directly from the third. Sooner or later, Christians (as they came to be called, first by their opponents,[48] then by themselves)[49] were thrown out of their local synagogues. It was their insistence that in his fulfilment of Israel's destiny Jesus had ended their ancient privileges so that henceforward anyone could come home to God through Christ, by passing the elaborate disciplines of Israel, which made the breach inevitable. And with the breach came other problems. The Jews had privileges at the court of Caesar as well as at that of God. By special dispensation they were exempted from offering incense to the 'divine' Emperor. That practice was as idolatrous and so as abhorrent to the Christians as it was to the Jews; but once the Christians were excluded from the Jewish fold they could no longer claim the exemption. It is probable that a large part of St Luke's motive in organizing the material for Acts as he did is to show the Roman authorities that St Paul, and before him St Peter, were acting in the true spirit of the Jewish faith in taking the line they did towards Gentiles which so scandalized the synagogue authorities. In the long run Christians would say he was correct: there is that in the Old Testament Scriptures which suggests that the fulfilment of Israel would lead to the opening of God's favour to all human beings; but in the short run he failed; and the result was persecution. The Church was illegal in the Empire.

The four changes just described may be called 'horizontal' for they concern the expansion of the Christian mission geographically and culturally. The fifth change is vertical in that it moves on the axis of time rather than space. The adjustments to be made were with the past and with the future which moved through the present into the past; it was above all the adjustment to death.

Part of the basic, almost unconscious, furniture of the mind which the Christians took over from their Jewish forerunners was a view of time as purposeful, developing, mounting to a climax. Time which meant history was the scene of God's activity. The line of human time was punctuated by crises where the purposes of God crossed it, often dramatically; for though they believed that 'God was working his purpose out as year succeeds to year', there were seasons of special intervention. The Christians believed that the most important crisis of divine intervention, the climax which they called the Kingdom of God, had come in with Jesus the Messiah, the Lord, the Son of God. They believed that he had inaugurated a new age, which was in fact the last age. There remained only the final climax, where that which was now private, hidden, revealed only to the few with eyes to see, would be made open and public. In that Last Day the divine purposes for the world would be wound up, God and his Christ and his people would be vindicated. The coming of the Holy Ghost at Pentecost had been taken as fulfilling the prophecy of Joel about the characteristics of the Last Day. It was not thought that there would be many years between Pentecost and the End. Meanwhile the work must continue for such time as might remain: proclaiming the salvation which God had provided through Jesus; offering, first to the Jew, then to the Gentile, a share in that salvation through repentance and faith; and building those who so accepted into local branches of God's New People, a community whose personal and corporate existence was styled by the Holy Spirit.

It was heady stuff. The New Testament exudes an excitement which is more easily caught from the modern translations. There was a proper urgency; there were some curious side-effects, especially within the churches that took root in pagan soil. The church at Thessalonica, for example, was not noted for its chastity. St Paul urged its members to live consistently with their faith, reminding them that 'the day of the Lord will come like a thief in the night', a basic point in the earliest Christian instruction. The result seems to have been unfortunate; some at least among the church there assumed that the Day had already arrived and, taking it that normal life should cease, stopped bothering to earn their living. St Paul had to send a stern word, again part of the basic teaching they had originally received: 'If anyone will not work, let him not eat.'[50] He also modified the programme of the End which he had given them, for apart from different imagery the account in the second letter to Salonika suggests a considerably longer period from that in the first letter,[51] though it still reads as though he expected it fairly soon. Similar considerations ('... I mean, brethren, the appointed time has grown very short') account for his much criticized teaching on marriage in the first letter to Corinth.[52] The letter to the Ephesians, written perhaps ten years later, contains very much more positive teaching about marriage[53] and the perspective in which St Paul looks at the long purposes of God has changed.[54]

It must have fairly soon become apparent that despite the startling initial success of the mission recorded in the early chapters of Acts, neither the Jewish nor the Roman world would capitulate to the claims of Christ. It seemed that the enemies were not merely human. The forces of evil were putting up a stiff rearguard action after their cosmic defeat in the death and resurrection of Christ. Images of warfare occur not only in the writings of St Paul but in almost all the New Testament literature; of warfare and of its stylized younger brother, the Roman public games. And as the infant Church settled down for a long haul, one problem became acute. What was to be the position of those Christians who died before Christ returned to reign in glory with his faithful people around him?

There had always been the risk of martyrdom. It caused no problem of belief. The earliest martyr, Stephen, had been comforted at the hour of his death by a vision of the Son of Man standing at the right hand of God: those who died for the cause would remain united with the Lord. But what of those who died in the natural course of events? Would they have lost their place among the victors when the day of victory dawned? No, St Paul reassured the Thessalonians who had raised the matter. If they were in Christ, then they would share in his resurrection whether or not they had died in the interval before his return. Indeed, they will enjoy a certain priority; for, when the Lord descends from heaven, 'the dead in Christ will rise first; then we who are alive who are left, shall be caught up together with them in the clouds to meet

the Lord in the air; and so we shall always be with the Lord. Therefore, comfort one another with these words.'[55] The implication is
that most Christians, including St Paul, were likely to be still
living.

It was probably a few years later when St Paul wrote his first
(surviving) letter to the brilliant, troublesome church at Corinth.
By that time many more Christians had died and he had reflected
further on the problem. His thoughts on how the resurrection of
Christ guarantees the resurrection of Christ's people are embodied
in the great fifteenth chapter that is prescribed to be read in the
Anglican burial service. The death of Christians is taken to be
normal. It is in the Corinthian correspondence that St Paul, perhaps
wearied by the constant cares of an apostle,[56] first shows his indiffer-
ence to the plots on his life; indeed there was a lot to be said for
death: 'While we are at home in the body we are away from the
Lord, for we walk by faith, not by sight. We are of good courage,
and we would rather be away from the body and at home with the
Lord. So whether we are at home or away, we make it our aim to
please him.'[57] By the time he wrote to the church at Philippi
from his imprisonment at Rome some years later, St Paul was even
more definite. 'For me to live is Christ and to die is gain', he wrote
in the course of asking prayer for his release from prison. 'If it is
to be life in the flesh, that means fruitful labour for me. Yet which
I shall choose I cannot tell. I am hard pressed between the two. My
desire is to depart and be with Christ, for that is far better. But to
remain in the flesh is more necessary on your account.'[58] From
that time onwards the death of Christians was taken as normal; we
shall consider shortly the place they had after their death in the
continuing struggles of God's people. The earlier and wider problem of the delay in Christ's return, too, came to be accepted as
normal by the end of the New Testament period. Some words from
the enigmatic writing attributed to St Peter as his second letter
set out the standard position. Answering those who were ridiculing
the Christian claim of the Lord's return, 'Peter' wrote: 'But do not
ignore this one fact, beloved, that with the Lord one day is as a
thousand years, and a thousand years as one day. The Lord is not
slow about his promise as some count slowness, but is forbearing
towards you, not wishing that any should perish, but that all should
reach repentance. But the day of the Lord will come as a thief....'[59]

One conviction of great importance had been cleared in the mind of the Church at a very early stage, which did much to ease the very real difficulty caused by the delay of the Lord's return and the consequent death of Christians: the position of those Old Testament figures who had looked for the coming of Christ. They were part of the same family, 'the fathers'. To say that the first Christians saw themselves as the true Israelites and so claimed the Old Testament Scriptures as their own, and that that self-understanding and that claim were not abandoned when the Church became predominantly Gentile, is true, but so understated as to mislead. It is too literary. In the same way the New Testament generation of Christians undoubtedly believed that many of the Scriptures pointed forward to the times of Jesus, foretelling the shape of things when Messiah came. But again, the relationship of prophecy and fulfilment, true though it is, does not express the full intimacy of the connection. The heroes of the Old Testament were heroes of the Christians as well as of the Jews because the God they had served was the Lord, God expressing himself through His eternal Son, the Word, the Protector and Deliverer of His people, the Messiah-to-be. The men of the New Testament found continuing kinship with the fathers of the Old Covenant because they in their several generations had encountered the pre-incarnate Christ, Jesus as he had been before the Word was made flesh. It was lasting relationship with God through him which determined lasting retationship between his people whether in this life or after it.

Since the position here maintained is unusual, it will be well to cite briefly four New Testament passages in support: two of them from apostolic writers, and two of them from recorded words of Jesus. In his first letter to Corinth, St Paul warns his readers against presuming upon God's favour as 'our fathers' had done in the time of Moses, when they were fed from manna and a hidden spring of water from a rock; 'and the rock was Christ.'[60] In St John's Gospel the evangelist, commenting on the people's unbelief despite the many signs which Jesus had done before them, quoted the prophet Isaiah. His second citation was from chapter 6, verse 10: 'He has blinded their eyes and hardened their heart, lest they should see with their eyes and perceive with their heart, and turn for me to heal them.' He adds some words which show that he was not thinking simply in terms of a prophecy fulfilled centuries after it was uttered. 'Isaiah said this because he saw his glory and spoke of him.' The vision of the Lord's glory which Isaiah saw 'in the year that King Uzziah died', which immediately preceded the prophecy St John quoted, was in fact a vision of the pre-incarnate Christ, or Jesus, as St John prefers to call him. Long before the Word had become flesh, 'He came to his own home and his own people received him not. But to all who received him, who believed in his name, he gave power to become children of God....'[61] St John would have us interpret the words he attributes to Jesus in controversy with the Jews, 'Your father Abraham rejoiced that he was to see my day',[62] much more literally than is usual. If we follow A. T. Hanson, who suggested in his book *Jesus Christ in the Old Testament*[63] that scholarship ought on its own terms to take more seriously this patristic approach as a clue to the New Testament interpretation of the Old, then St Luke's statement that the risen Christ, 'beginning with Moses and all the prophets, interpreted to them in all the scriptures the things concerning himself' takes on additional meaning.

IV

We have now set the scene for interpreting one of the most remarkable elements in early Christian experience. It is classically expressed in the Epistle to the Hebrews in the opening sentence of chapter 12: 'Therefore, since we are surrounded by so great a cloud of witnesses, let us also lay aside every weight, and sin which clings so closely, and let us run with perseverance the race that is set before us, looking to Jesus the pioneer and perfecter of our faith, who for the joy that was set before him endured the cross, despising the shame, and is seated at the right hand of the throne of God.' We may call this experience 'the encouragement of heavenly supporters'.

The imagery is evidently that of the Roman public games. Christians are pictured as athletes. If they are to succeed they must divest themselves of superfluous flesh, which in practice means sin. The race is a hard one and to keep going they must fix their eyes on Jesus. In fact, the imagery is not too precise; it seems to oscillate between the race and the fight with gladiators or with beasts. But throughout it is an image of the Christian struggle. It is the spectators on whom we must concentrate. The 'therefore' which introduces the exhortation is a very emphatic one. The spectators who, continuing the image, are thronging the seats of the amphitheatre provide the very reason for the Christians to step their efforts up to the maximum.

Commentators stress that these spectators are described in an unexpected word. It is the Greek original of the English word 'martyr'. It is not absolutely impossible for it to mean 'spectator', though for that one would have expected the Greek word which gives us the English 'theatre'. The point is important though negative conclusions are unwarranted. The witnesses who surround the struggling Christians are indeed spectators. But they are not spectators with the detached, even hostile, attitude of those who usually watch the games. They are there because they are themselves witnesses to that to which the Christians in their struggle are now witnessing. They are the witnesses to Jesus as he was before the days of his flesh, the witnesses of the Old Testament.

The emphatic 'therefore' shows how closely we should connect the passage with what precedes it. Chapter 11 begins with a specific and unusual definition of faith: 'The assurance of things hoped for, the conviction of things not seen'. The writer goes on to give a roll of honour, listing the men and women of faith, with a note of those actions of theirs which pleased God. The persons listed—and many others, for whose recalling time, the author says, failed him—all died in faith 'not having received what was promised, but having seen it and greeted it from afar....'[64] The emphasis on faith 'without which it is impossible to please God' and on the promises which the faithful people died without receiving suggest strongly that it is the Christian gospel which is meant: that is, the assurance of being accepted with God by faith in Jesus and his sacrifice—the latter, of course, the main theological theme of the epistle. The suggestion becomes almost a certainty with the explanation the author gives of why the ancient men of faith failed to receive the promises: 'Since God had foreseen something better for us that apart from us they should not be made perfect.'[65] The spectators were thus those who in their own day had been engaged in the life-and-death struggle being presently carried on by the Christian Church. Even though they had not been able to see clearly, they were none the less witnesses to Jesus. As much as the Christians now, in their own day and degree the fathers were acceptable to God because of their faith; and they now came to see the fulfilment of it all, surrounding their successors in the new generation's struggle on earth and with them looking to Jesus the pioneer and perfector of the faith which marked both spectators and contestants.

Two questions immediately come to mind. Are we to think of the cloud of witnesses as an exercise in recollection for the contestants—remember the heroes of old and take courage—or should we think of them as being in some way actually present and actively encouraging? And secondly, what bearing has this 'cloud of witnesses' from Old Testament times on the matter of relationships between Christians now living and those who have died from the time of St Stephen to our own? Before attempting to answer directly these most important questions, however, it will be well to look again at 'the people of Jesus' and see what the inquiry so far has added to our understanding of that 'people' and its features.

In the previous chapter we located the heart of the people in the disciples gathered loyally round their teacher. We then found that four factors exercised their full influence in modifying this picture by the time that the New Testament documents had been written. Their effect had been to change the little group of Palestine Jews into a worldwide religion open to Jew and Gentile alike. Jesus, removed from view by his return to the Father, was being made present in a manner unbounded by space, so that in spite of the massive dispersal of his disciples, they were still able to meet with him in their midst. The fifth factor of change, which had not fully exerted its influence by the time the New Testament period closed, was concerned with time rather than with space. The arrival of Jesus as a human being had not been the arrival of a total stranger. It was rather the full focusing into human life of the Son, or Word, or Wisdom, of God, the divine Spirit who as long as there had been a creation had been involved in its developing process; who had made himself known in a great variety of ways to the nation which among all the nations of the world had been selected to bear that knowledge (which is not to say that there was no knowledge of him outside its boundaries). We have in this chapter looked at a particular New Testament passage where the embattled people of Jesus were urged to take heart from the great cloud surrounding them of those who, under the Old Covenant, had witnessed to the same

Lord who now since the days of his flesh might be so much more clearly discerned.

The people of Jesus is thus a fellowship of loyalty to him which transcends time as well as space; which finds its centre of loyalty and its source of succour in him who transcends time and space; and which is bound into one by the Spirit who creates loyalty between those who look to him, however separated they may be by time as well as by space.

The network of relationships called into being between Christ and those who have put their trust in him is unique; there is thus no human association to compare it with. A great many phrases occur in the New Testament, each of which describes the Church from some particular point of view. Paul S. Minear, in his modern classic *Images of the Church in the New Testament*[66] lists thirty-two 'minor images' and four great clusters: the People of God; the New Creation; the Fellowship in Faith; and the Body of Christ. His analysis of them and their interrelations occupies over 250 pages of densely packed, and very enlightening, exposition. Minear's book was one of many called forth by the ecumenical movement and the new urgency which that movement has given to all Christian bodies to review their understanding of themselves in the light of origins which they all share. Clearly the present work cannot contribute directly to this important debate; we can only draw upon its findings where they illustrate our theme.

Of Minear's major images we have used mostly the first and the third. We shall discuss the third, the New Creation, shortly. We must now consider certain aspects of his fourth one. Like all the other 'great' images, that of the Body of Christ is not one complete image but a cluster of related word-pictures, used, not necessarily consistently with each other, to illustrate a particular face of Christian existence which circumstances have called into prominence. It is therefore most unwise to build images into doctrines. But what does run through the 'Body of Christ' cluster is the element of solidarity. Relationships established with Christ place the individuals concerned in an association whose growth is powered by the Spirit so that it may be described in quasi-organic language. To be a 'member of Christ' is a different kind of belonging to being a member of a sailing club. You do not pay your subscription to the Association, with the threat of lapsing if it is not renewed.

The Association, on the contrary, supplies you with its own life. A 'member' of Christ means a 'limb' of his. We are 'in' him and he is 'in' us: there is a mutuality of indwelling which binds its members into a solidarity as unbreakable as our membership of the human race, a solidarity which is basically given and to which only in the second place do we contribute.

The solidarity of which Christians find themselves members is therefore one into whose ongoing life they are caught up so as to be penetrated by it, and ultimately transformed. It is a solidarity which stretches back at least as far as the call of Abraham. The full definition of this solidarity took place when the Word of God was made flesh and in his human flesh lived, died, was raised from the dead and returned to his eternal glory, leaving his presence within the created order to be known through the Spirit given at a new intensity. It is a solidarity, therefore, which implies resurrection of its members, to whom death has become incidental to their ultimate destiny.

But death is still an incident, and one which looms very large from the human standpoint. From the eternal standpoint, where time does not exist, death is no doubt already swallowed up in the victory of the resurrection; but for all human beings, creatures within time, the resurrection of the dead lies in the future; it awaits the return of the Lord. Those bald statements, made after the earlier treatment of the solidarity which has its centre in Christ, indicate the uncertainty which has made the relations between the living and the departed one of the most divisive areas of Christian belief. It is the area where the Catholic Church of the Middle Ages elaborated the doctrine of purgatory as an antechamber to heaven where redeemed souls worked out temporal satisfaction for their sins, preparing themselves thereby for the vision of God which would have blinded them had they been exposed to it in the penitent but unsanctified state in which they had died. It is the area where Reformed Christians, reacting against the calculating quality in the catholicism of their day, with its prescriptions of masses, prayers, indulgences, and other devices by which the faithful of the day could offer to shorten the purgatorial discipline, denied all possibility of contact between the living and the departed; the only true comfort lay in the assurance that all who had in their lifetime trusted in Christ were after their death at peace 'in him'. And it is the area where countless moderns have either quietly opted out, disbelieving in any personal life after death—many such are to be found in the churches as well as among the unchurched; or have had recourse to spiritualism, reincarnation, or other doctrines and practices strange to the Christian tradition.

As so often in healing the divided mind of Western Christendom, the way ahead is to go behind the hardened attitudes of Reformation and Counter-Reformation and to try to see the positive truth which both were seeking, in as undeformed a state as possible. Our immediate task, therefore, is to connect the solidarity which Christ's people belong to with the doctrine of the Communion of Saints. We may start from a modern spokesman for the conservative Prostestant tradition. Writing in the 'Christian Foundations' series, J. A. Motyer asks in his book *After Death*:[67]

> But what of 'the communion of saints'? How are we still one with those who have gone on? There are two aspects of this: we are one in Christ, and we are one in expectation of Christ. Some sort of comparison can be drawn in respect of Christians who have gone to the other side of the world in Christ's service. Our continuing oneness with them is entirely Christ-centred: there is oneness in loving the same Lord; there is oneness in continuing to love one another with that characteristic love which only Christians know; and, since they are still in the body, there is oneness of concern issuing in mutual prayer. This is 'the communion of saints' and, apart from the last matter, our oneness with departed Christians is exactly the same.

Many will feel that by his 'apart from the last matter' Mr Motyer has not only destroyed the profoundest point of the comparison he has made, otherwise an excellent one, but also emptied the doctrine of the Communion of Saints of all meaning (his use both of lower-case letters and of inverted commas will not escape attention). But it would do no service to the cause of Christian unity to dismiss his arguments as those of a Protestantism too negative to warrant further attention. He writes from a universe of convictions which is Protestant in the high sense of speaking on behalf of gospel truths. It is true that of the ten pages allocated in his book to the chapter headed 'The Communion of Saints', only two, under the sub-heading 'Oneness in Christ' are on that subject; the other subheadings in the chapter are 'Spiritualism', 'Uncertainty', 'Spiritual Danger', 'The Resurrection', and (after 'Oneness in Christ') 'Waiting'. But the whole is set in the context of the first chapter headed 'The Love that drew Salvation's Plan', and the last one entitled 'Jesus Christ our Lord'. In other words, the negative attitude towards Christian relationships across the barrier of death is caused by a desire to exalt the gospel which discloses the grand designs of God for sinful mankind. It is misleading to dismiss his view of the part without regard to his understanding of the whole. Nor should one dismiss his 'Protest' as belonging only to the sixteenth century and to the deformations of Catholic doctrine then prevailing.

It will nevertheless be useful to set beside Mr Motyer's remarks those of a spokesman for the Christian tradition which has not known, except marginally, the phenomena of deformation,[68] Reformation and Counter-Reformation, the Eastern Orthodox Church. 'In God and His Church', writes Kallistos Ware, 'there is no division between the living and the departed, but all are one in the love of the Father. Whether we are alive or whether we are dead, as members of the Church we still belong to the same family, and still have a duty to bear one another's burdens. Therefore just as Orthodox Christians here on earth pray for one another and ask for one another's prayers, so they pray also for the faithful departed and ask the faithful departed to pray for them. Death cannot sever the bond of mutual love which links the members of the Church together.'[69] Father Ware's statement seems to me a more natural consequence of the relationships we found in the evidence that Mr Motyer's.

One of the principal Protestant difficulties over prayer across the divide of death is to understand what may be permissibly prayed for the dead. This present life was the scene for decision: choices made here decided once and for all whether in its inmost bent a soul was destined for heaven or for hell. All but those liberal Protestants who have severed their links with historic Christianity agree that no prayers can avail for those unhappy (and possibly rare) souls who in their lifetime had opted against God and good and life. In his chapter 'Can We Help?' Mr Motyer deals with the matter entirely in terms of the Reformation and its issues. He equates prayer for the dead with prayer for the shortening of their time in purgatory, and by purgatory he understands essentially the place or state of self-expiation. He bases his argument largely on the third part of the Sermon concerning Prayer in the Anglican *Book of Homilies*,[70] which was first published in 1562 and is an important part of the official English statement of protest against medieval abuses. 'If we will cleave only unto the Word of God,' the Homily runs, 'then we must needs grant that we have no commandment ... to pray for the dead.'[71] There being no purgatory, 'the dead are either in paradise where they do not need our prayers, or else are under divine judgement, in which case our prayers are of no avail', is how Mr Motyer summarizes the Homily's teaching.[72]

The conception of prayer contained in the Protestant objection seems to be as deformed by legalistic assumptions as the doctrines associated with purgatory to which it is opposed. Is prayer in this life concerned only with its object's transference from damnation to salvation? Do Christians not pray for each other on the grounds that they are already 'in Christ' and so do not need prayer? Mr Motyer's admirable illustration from missionary prayer shows that he does not think so. He and the evangelical tradition he represents are well aware of the rich consequences in prayer which come from shared acceptance of the gospel. One would have supposed it enhanced rather than diminished by death 'in Christ'. The living do not pray for the departed in specific petitions, for we do not know their needs as we know those of our living contemporaries. The traditional prayers concern their rest, repose, and refreshment. There is room for improvement here, and one of the reasons why prayer for the departed is so neglected is the failure of generally accepted forms to stress sufficiently the delight we have in our oneness with those whose experience of Christ so far surpasses our own. Prayer in the Body of Christ is essentially communion with each other and the Lord. Prayer with the departed is an expression of our mutuality; making prayer for them, sharing prayer with them, receiving the help of their prayers—replace the legalism of medieval deformations by a fresh experience of what it means to be among Christ's people and those distinctions lose their importance. Such liberty in prayer is a part of the gospel for whose neglect the Protestant world is much the poorer.

The mutual sharing and caring in Christ for one another is the life-blood of the solidarity to which we belong. The heavenly supporters who formed so great a cloud of witnesses in the first Christian century have since been enormously increased. But the solidarity is not simply one of size, but of holiness. It consists of individuals whose personalities are being suffused and transformed by the Holy Spirit until their wills and desires and delights are wholly one with Christ's. To risk a diagram, we may picture those at the centre in whom this process has been most fully completed. The rich shade of glory gets paler as the circle widens to its periphery where we are caught up into the solidarity. Here the grace and the glory are still mainly external, for justification has not yet led on to deep penetration by holiness and so the angularities and possessiveness of individualism have not matured far into the joys of interdependence. But grace has evoked the basic response and however distressing the stumblings and the failures, we are sustained by the Spirit working through the hugeness of the whole Christ to whom we belong.

V

Within the solidarity that centres upon Christ, his mother holds a special place. In the order of God's purposes in history, she was the one in whose body the pre-existent Son, in whom all things hold together,[73] took human flesh upon himself. She is therefore the climax of the Old Testament people, the one to whom the cloud of witnesses from the ancient era look as their crowning glory, for it was through her response to grace that their Vindicator came to stand upon the earth.[74] In the order of redemption, she is the first-fruits of her Son's saving work, the one among her Son's people who has gone all the way. And in the order of her Son's people, she is the mother. We go on now to see the implications of that statement.

Mary's motherhood is essentially theological; not, as might appear from much debased devotion in painting, hymns, and prayers, sentimental. The fundamental reason for paying her special attention, it cannot be too often stressed, is that she is *Theotokos*, the Mother of God.[75] We have had occasion several times already to turn from the controversies of the Western churches to the East, with its tradition that has developed relatively undisturbed by theological controversy. 'In Orthodox services', writes Father Ware,[76] 'Mary is often mentioned, and on each occasion she is usually given her full title: "Our All-Holy, immaculate, most blessed and glorified

Lady, Mother of God and Ever-Virgin Mary." Here are included the three chief epithets applied to our Lady by the Orthodox Church: *Theotokos* ..., *Aeiparthenos* (Ever-Virgin), and *Panagia* (All-Holy)....' We must examine the last two.

This is not the place to discuss the historical and exegetical questions about the 'brothers of the Lord', and the precise nature of their kinship to Jesus.[77] There is certainly nothing in the Scriptures to invalidate the conclusion of the Church in the days before the split between East and West that Mary was a virgin all her life, after the birth of Jesus as well as before it.[78] The perpetual virginity of Mary has great importance for our understanding of her position in the purposes of God, as well in the consequences of his Son's incarnation as in the manner of it. This importance is a positive one, and has nothing to do with an exaggerated asceticism which consigns sexuality to the undesirable parts of human existence. We saw earlier[79] that in relation to the birth of Jesus, his mother's virginity was 'to be understood primarily as a witness to the unique relation of this man to God since he had no father except God'.[80]

Mary's perpetual virginity has great importance, too, for her place and her ministry among her Son's people. It is first of all a sign to remind them that they are a pilgrim people, not a settled one. Here they have no lasting city, so they do not drive down the roots of settled family life: the reproach which Mary suffered[81] is a reproach constantly made against the Church by 'committed' politicians and idealists of one hue or another for its failure to back unreservedly any particular programme of action. In Father Jelly's words, 'As the type of all that Christ's Pilgrim Church is called to become and to experience, Mary's virginity is the model for the virginal spouse of Christ who is to beget his life among men spiritually.'[82] It is a 'sign'; not merely an exhortation, but a witness by example; more intimately, by microcosmic fulfilment, for as we saw in our examination of the early Jerusalem icon, Mary is in herself the representative Church.[83]

A further significance of Mary's perpetual virginity to her distinctive place among her Son's people lies in the way it has realized the possibility of love without possessiveness. Father Jelly calls it 'the eschatological significance of the sharing fully in Christ's glory when there will be no marriage'.[84] The reference is to the incident recorded in all the Synoptic Gospels.[85] The Sadducees, who said that there was no resurrection (so like sophisticated moderns) had asked Jesus which of seven brothers, six of whom had successively and very properly married the widow of the first, would be her husband when the resurrection came. The question was a false one, Jesus replied, for marriage is an institution which belongs to this present life. It is desirable, and necessary, and in every way honourable; but it has about it the taint of exclusiveness, of possessiveness, which is proper to this life but which has no place in the life of the world to come. In this life 'free love' is impossible without licentiousness; but in the life to come the selfish elements, predatory, exclusive, and exploitive, will have been purged away so that in the general interchange of charity the safeguards of marriage will have become redundant. In our present existence, this truth may be distantly glimpsed in the successful realization of the rare vocation to celibacy, where the energies of love are set free for general disbursement by the disclaiming of exclusive relationship. Its full glory may be seen in the person of our Lord and his universal love which all could claim and receive but none could monopolize. In this sphere of love's freedom Mary enjoys to the full an identification with him which is ultimately open to all his people as their sanctification reaches its full term. It has set her free for the universal ministry among her Son's people which we will shortly describe.

Mary's perpetual virginity thus formed part of her all-holiness; which is not to say that celibacy is holier than marriage, as is the vulgar inference from such a statement, but that in her case holiness increased along the path of virginity. Vladimir Lossky, in a most valuable paper entitled *Panagia*,[86] related the special holiness of Mary to the two occasions when she received the Holy Spirit. He drew an analogy with the two descents of the Spirit upon the apostles, according to St John on Easter evening, and according to St Luke on the day of Pentecost. The Johannine account stressed the functional nature of the Spirit's coming: it was for the power of binding and loosing. The Pentecostal coming was for the fulfilment of personal qualities. So the descent upon Mary at the Annunciation was for the purpose of the Incarnation; but the descent upon her at Pentecost was for her personal sanctification. 'But the two communications of the Spirit, that which is functional and that which is personal, are mutually complementary', wrote Professor Lossky. '...
The two should coincide more and more as life goes on; one's

function (or vocation) normally becomes a way by which one acquires selflessness and personal sanctity.' Thus, for Mary, 'the objective function of her divine maternity, in which she was placed on the day of her Annunciation, will be her personal way of sanctification. She will realize in her consciousness the meaning of the fact of her having carried in her womb and having nourished at her breast the Son of God'. 'So it is', says Professor Lossky, 'that the sayings in the Gospels which seem to depreciate her at the expense of the disciples[87] ... receive their true meaning as words spoken in supreme praise of her; blessed is she who not only was the Mother of God but also realized in her own person the degree of holiness corresponding to that unique function. The person of the Mother of God is exalted more than her function, and the completion of her holiness receives more praise than its beginning.'[88]

Mary of Nazareth, the All-Holy and Ever-Virgin Mother of God, finds her most distinctive place among her Son's people as the mother. It is no doubt her closeness to her Son, both physically and spiritually, which makes possible her motherhood in the full sense. For, as we have seen, she is not merely an individual, she is the Church represented in the disciple who has gone all the way: the type of Mother Church as well as a mother in the Church. It is her motherhood which accounts for her distinctive ministry towards her fellow-members of her Son's people; and here, unfortunately, we meet the greatest controversies.

The account of the wedding at Cana can give us an outline of her maternal ministry. We looked at St John's account earlier[89] in our examination of Mary as her Son's disciple; we return to it to see what it can tell us about her ministry. We saw before the crucial importance of the fact that the 'hour' of Jesus had not then come. That Mary's intervention in the contretemps at the wedding was, in the order of gospel events, premature, is no obstacle in the way of drawing from it the outlines of her eventual ministry; for the principle of simultaneity which we have detected in St John's presentation of the truth that came by Jesus[90] means that at one level the incident is to be read in the light of the further episode involving Mary at the foot of the cross.

Max Thurian's comments are particularly helpful. Making the point which we earlier noted, that Mary's faith and obedience preceded the faith and obedience of both the servants and the disciples,

Thurian shows that by her instruction to the servants, 'Do whatever he tells you', Mary 'shares in the spiritual motherhood of the Church which, by the Word of Christ, gives birth to the sons of the Father in heaven by causing them to be born by faith and obedience'. Furthermore, Mary's spiritual motherhood is exercised in the contagious quality of her own faith: that faith, which is 'total abandon to the will and word of Christ ("Whatsoever he says"), communicates itself to the servants ("... do it"), and precedes and prepares for the glory of the Messiah which will awaken faith in the disciples ("... and the disciples believed in him"). Mary here fulfils the ministry of communicating the faith, she gives birth to the faith of others, and shares in the motherhood of the Church.'[91]

The motherhood of the Church is unfamiliar to many Christians as a serious concept, and some words of explanation will be in place. It is one of the many areas of Christian truth where speech has to be in metaphor, and where the pressing of a single metaphor to its logical conclusion is almost bound to result in distortion. Contrary to the grammarian's advice, in matters of theology there is safety in the mixed metaphor; many of the subjects we are concerned with, since only a part of them lies within common human experience, can only be spoken about in a number of metaphors, each of which illustrates some part of the truth, none of which can of itself convey the whole. Thus St Paul, the principal elaborator of the Church's motherhood, writes to the Galatians: 'My little children, with whom I am again in travail until Christ be formed in you!' The expression is wrung from the apostle in a moment of affectionate exasperation with the wayward Galatian Christians. A few sentences later, in a careful analysis of the choices confronting them (and their present conduct indicates that they are in danger of making an irrevocably wrong choice) in terms of the two sons of Abraham, he speaks of the Church as 'Jerusalem above, which is free, and the mother of us all'.[92] But the metaphor is capable of startling variations. St Paul can see himself in relation to the churches he has founded not only as a mother, but as a father.[93]

A remark of Max Thurian's shows the consistency beneath the verbal contradictions of these Pauline metaphors. 'In all these cases the conversion to Christ by faith is seen as a giving birth by the ministry of the Word of God, a giving birth by Mother Church, in whose motherhood the Apostle takes his part.'[94]

Such is the context in which we should try to understand the Roman Catholic teaching on the Virgin's part in human salvation. 'The maternal duty of Mary towards men in no way obscures or diminishes ... [the] unique mediation of Christ,' declared the Vatican Fathers,[95] 'but rather shows his power.' Anything Mary did by way of mediation depended on what her Son did and was in every way secondary and derivative. But at the foot of the cross she 'united herself with a maternal heart to His sacrifice, and lovingly consented to the immolation of this Victim which she herself had brought forth.' I have elsewhere expressed some hesitation over the exegesis of the biblical texts which underly this assertion of *De Ecclesia* (chapter 58).[96] Mary, the argument runs, shared fully in the redemptive purpose of her Son. It was for that reason that from the cross he appointed her to be the mother 'in the order of grace'.[97]

The identity of purpose with her Son which St John indicates, and the intercession shown in the Acts, did not cease when Mary was taken up into heaven. 'By her maternal charity', agreed the Vatican Fathers, 'she cares for the brethren of her Son, who still journey on earth surrounded by dangers and difficulties, until they are led into the happiness of their true home. Therefore the blessed virgin is invoked by the Church under the titles of advocate, auxiliatrix, adjutrix, and mediatrix.'[98] There follows a qualification of these terms to avoid suggesting any parity between Mary and her Son, 'for no creature could ever be counted as equal with the incarnate Word and redeemer'. We shall examine this disclaimer shortly.

Meanwhile the argument continues to relate Mary's motherhood of the Redeemer to her motherhood of the redeemed. 'As St Ambrose taught, the mother of God is a type of the Church in the order of faith, charity, and perfect union with Christ. For in the mystery of the Church, which is itself rightly called mother and virgin, the blessed virgin stands out in eminent and singular fashion as exemplar both of virgin and mother.' She is the new Eve; a matter to which our next chapter is devoted. 'The Son whom she brought forth is he whom God placed as the first-born among many brethren (cf. Rom.8.29), namely the faithful, in whose birth and education she co-operates with a maternal love.'[99] Here, Mary's maternal function is the Church's maternal function particularized; the nature of and the reason for that particularization spring from the fact of Mary's being (in our terminology, not that of the Vatican Fathers) the one of her Son's people who has 'arrived'.[100]

A striking feature of the Council's Mariological teaching is that it is so firmly centred on her Son. Mary exists and is honoured for him, not for herself. Her maternal role is essentially that of helping her Son's people, in the Church or beyond it, into obedience to him. Her ministry is subordinate to his by intention as well as because of her total creatureliness. The Protestant's worst fears of the Blessed Virgin's advancement to the Godhead find no food for growth in the *Constitution on the Church*. Pope Paul's proclamation that Mary is 'Mother of the Church', though greeted with some alarm at the time because it seemed to show that the Council had not really checked the runaway tendencies in recent Mariology, in fact added nothing to what the Council had said; it merely relieved the worries of the more conservative Catholics by spelling out what the Council had left implicit. 'The title', wrote Dom Ralph Russell, a biblical theologian noted for his generous ecumenism and who had much to do in advising the Vatican Fathers in Marian matters, 'therefore remains outside the *Constitution* but proclaimed separately by the Pope. Mary is both a member of the Mystical Body and the mother of the other members of the family: "She holds the loftiest position in the Church after Christ, and the nearest to us" (Pope Paul).'[101]

The evangelical who stresses that the Church is above all the family of God into which, thanks to the sacrifice of Christ, believing sinners are adopted, can surely lose nothing and gain a great deal from realizing his relationship to Mary as his mother in the order of grace. But a word must be said further about the notion of Mary as mediatrix; for, despite the disclaimers of the Council, it is precisely here that suspicions of a Marian 'takeover' of the Christian faith reach their zenith. It has to be admitted that there is a great deal in everyday Catholic practice which causes alarm. There is the impression which Anglo-Saxons especially gain from visits to Catholic churches during holidays in Latin countries or in Ireland; as I have written elsewhere, 'The evangelical cannot but be impressed by what he sees in Roman churches: the blaze of candles throwing into relief shadowy figures praying before the statue of our Lady, while our Lord in the Blessed Sacrament is by comparison deserted.'[102] Perhaps underlying that phenomenon, and if so, all the worse, is the view that Mary is somehow easier to get round than her Son; if you can get in with her, a good word will be whispered in the right quarter which will stand you in good stead when the time comes. One has indeed heard rumours of a refinement in this travesty of Christian faith, whereby an approach to St Anne, by tradition the mother of the Blessed Virgin, is held to be advisable before tackling the Blessed Virgin herself. The possibilities of regression thereby opened up would seem to extend from the Second Eve to the First; one has only to state such views for their absurdity as well as their deplorable theology to be exposed. Yet, supposing for a moment that views of this kind do exist in some areas of Catholic life, could it be said that a determined researcher could not uncover similar perversions of Christian truth within Protestant churches?

It is not the horror stories of the worst that can be found which need to be faced in serious ecumenism, but the implications of Catholicism at its best. Is not the assertion of even a subordinate mediatorship on Mary's part an unwarrantable infringement on the unique mediatorship of her Son? I believe that it is not. My reasons spring from the fact that Mary's mediatorship arises from the ministry she has been given and not from her own virtues. Her role, as we have just seen, is to point not to herself but to her Son. In that respect Mary stands in the line of all genuine Christian ministry. For the fact remains that, though there are notable exceptions to which the Bible Societies especially bear witness, in most cases it takes a human being (or a collection of human beings gathered in a 'church') to mediate Christ to those who have not previously realized him as being of any vital concern to themselves. Christ is indeed the only mediator between God and man; but Christian experience shows no limit in the number of mediators needed between Christ and man.

The theologian interpreting the historian's estimate of Christian experience at that point will no doubt insist that the human mediators were functioning not as external powers but in their own true nature as members and agents of Christ, the one and only true Mediator; and so, too, we wish to insist, it is with the subordinate mediation of Mary, mediatrix. To assert her function as mediatrix in no way sets her up as an independent and rival source of mediation; it defines more closely her Son's mediatorship and the way it works. Much of what is said about her could be said of anyone engaged in the ministry of evangelism or of intercession. The spiritual authority of such persons derives not from their own excellence but from the way in which it pleases God through his Holy Spirit to use them in drawing human beings to Himself through Christ. The sub-mediation (if the term may be permitted) of the mother of God, or of any of the saints, living or departed, may differ in degree, but it does not differ in kind. Its efficacy is derived from that of 'the one mediator between God and men, the man Christ Jesus, who gave himself as a ransom for all, the testimony to which was borne at the proper time'.[103]

It is for this reason that Protestants may, with no violence to their fundamental convictions, ally themselves with the supplications of the mother of God as well as with those of such of their contemporaries as they wish, for the furtherance of their efforts in the gospel. And what is true of the mother of God is true of all the saints.

VI

'In the eastern apse' of an Orthodox church, writes Dr Nicolas Zernov,[104] 'the most significant place after the dome, stands the Virgin Mother, the link between the Creator and the creation. The Mother of God is the mother of all mankind, the friend and protectress of all members of the Church.' Dr Zernov's account of the position her icon occupies in the church buildings of his tradition introduces well the theme of Mary as the second Eve, where her motherhood reaches its climax, extending widely enough to include the whole human race.

In an historical study of Christian reflection upon Mary, this theme should have come first, for it was the earliest teaching about the mother of Jesus to be developed. Logically, too, it might have been the best place to start. Paul F. Palmer, the editor of a useful little volume of extracts giving the key Marian doctrines from the earliest times to 1950, tells how the theme of the second Eve 'developed with ever-unfolding variations in what may be called the Church's symphonic hymn to Mary'; he believes that all the doctrinal elaboration concerning the Blessed Virgin are latent within it.[105] A few examples from the early Christian writers will show its main features.

It was St Justin the Martyr in the middle of the second century who wrote the earliest account of the parallel which has survived. It comes in his *Dialogue with Trypho*, a book aimed at convincing Jewish readers that the claims made for Jesus are true. 'The First-born of the Father is born of the Virgin', wrote Justin,

> in order that the disobedience caused by the serpent might be destroyed in the same manner in which it had originated. For Eve, an undefiled virgin, conceived the word of the serpent, and brought forth disobedience and death. But the Virgin Mary, filled with faith and joy, when the angel Gabriel announced to her the good tidings that the Spirit of the Lord would come upon her, and the power of the Highest would overshadow her, and therefore the Holy One to be born of her would be the Son of God, answered: 'Be it done unto me according to thy word' (Luke 1.35). And, indeed, she gave birth to Him, concerning whom we have shown so many passages of Scripture were written, and by whom God destroys both the serpent and those angels and men who have become like the serpent, but frees from death those who repent of their sins and believe in Christ.[106]

Mary's reversal of Eve's disastrous action is expressed variously. St Irenaeus a generation later than Justin stressed the restoration of balance: 'As the human race was sentenced to death by means of a virgin, so it is now set aright by means of a virgin. The balance is restored to equilibrium: a virgin's disobedience is saved by a virgin's obedience.'[107] His younger contemporary, the North African lawyer Tertullian, sees it in terms of two contrasting words and the results of accepting them.

> For into Eve, as yet a virgin, had crept the devil's word, the framer of death. Equally, into a virgin was introduced God's word, the builder of life: so that what had been lost through one sex might by the same sex be restored and saved. Eve had believed the serpent, Mary believed Gabriel. The fault which the one committed by believing, by believing the other amended.[108]

A century and a half later, the Syrian poet-theologian, St Ephrem, makes Mary's role as the second Eve a central theme in his verse; for example:

Eve wrote in Eden the great handwriting of debt whereby her posterity should pass on death to all generations; the serpent signed the fatal book, sealed and secured it with the signet of fraud. Eve brought on the sin, and the debt was reserved for the Virgin Mary, that she might pay the debts of her mother, and tear up the handwriting under which were groaning all generations.... Two virgins there were, but of these two, very different was the conduct: the one laid prostrate her husband, the other uplifted her father. Through Eve man found his grave, through Mary he was called to heaven.[109]

Were those early Christian writers introducing a note unheard of in the faith of the apostles' own age, taking the first step on a path which would seriously distort the true Christian faith? David F. Wells clearly thinks that they were, though the fact that he dates the rise of the doctrine from the fifth century, when St Jerome 'observed that when the angelic greeting of Luke 1.28 is converted into Latin (*Ave Maria*) and the *ave* is then spelled backwards, one has the Latin for Eve (*Eva*) ...' does not suggest a very close study of the subject. Dr Wells supposes that it was the change of gender in Genesis 3.15, from 'he shall crush his heel' to 'she shall crush her heel' in the Latin translation of the Hebrew, which gave rise to the parallel; but we have seen it in Greek writings two or three centuries earlier than Jerome. Dr Wells finds it objectionable to call Mary the second Eve on the grounds that Scripture does not do so, and that the implied comparison with Christ as the Last Adam associates her not only in representing mankind but in our salvation; we have already considered this matter in the previous chapter.[110]

Two things in general may be said. First, there is certainly no explicit mention of the parallel within the canon of New Testament writings; and second, the very strong New Testament emphasis on Christ as the New or Last Adam meant that the parallel between Eve and Mary was a natural and straightforward development for the Christian mind to make as it reflected on the Scriptures. It was 'congruous'; but we are rightly suspicious of a theological argument which starts by saying 'it could be', goes on to say 'it was suitable for it to be', and finishes by saying 'and so it was'. Dr Alan Richardson has examined the matter carefully in his *Introduction to the Theology of the New Testament*.[111] The one place where the parallel might be implied is in the Revelation to St John the Divine, in that highly allusive and mysterious passage in chapter 12 where the 'woman arrayed with the sun' gives birth to 'a son, a male child'. The primary reference is clearly to the Jewish Church which gives birth to Christ and becomes the Jewish Christian community. But there is a reference in verse 17 to the war between the dragon or serpent and the seed of the woman which certainly alludes to the prophecy made to Eve in Genesis 3.15. Double symbolism is frequent in the Apocalypse; and the woman, according to Dr Richardson, 'may well represent both the Jewish Church and Eve-Mary.... But it can hardly be said that the parallel between Eve and Mary is clear beyond doubt: we find a hint rather than an assertion of it.' Yet, whether or not it was drawn by the New Testament writers, 'the parallel', Dr Richardson concludes, 'is real enough.'

To see why an understanding of Mary as the second Eve is no mere academic nicety or literary flourish, but has great consequences for our understanding of the Christian gospel especially as the good news in our own time, it will be helpful to examine the figure of Eve as she appears in the book called Genesis. We shall approach the familiar narratives of chapters 2 and 3 along paths suggested by recent studies in Old Testament theology. Those who have a knowledge of this subject will recognize the debt that I owe to the great German scholar Gerhard von Rad;[112] though of course he is not to be blamed for my opinions.

Everybody knows that the Book Genesis carries two accounts of the creation of the human species. We read in chapter 1 that 'God created man in his own image, in the image of God created he him: male and female created he them.[113] That statement says two things: that the species is unlike the rest of the creation which has just been described, for it is made in the 'image of God'; and that it is created in two sexes. Scholars call the narrative of chapter 1 the 'priestly' account and connect its author with the time of the Jewish Exile in Babylon.

It is only necessary to read aloud the first two chapters of Genesis to hear the change of approach which comes in the middle of chapter 2, verse 4. The observant reader will confirm the scholar's finding that the term used to speak of the Creator changes: He is God in chapter 1, and the LORD GOD in chapter 2. The name of the Creator is not the only difference between the two accounts. The second narrative is more diffuse and more detailed. In place of chapter I succinct statement of human origins, the second narrative tells three stories. The LORD GOD forms man out of the dust of the ground and breathes upon him, whereupon he becomes a living being. The LORD GOD then puts him into a garden to till it, and allows him to eat of every three he finds there except one. And, thirdly, the LORD GOD decides that the man should not be alone. He forms the animals out of the ground first of all, and brings them in turn to the man. The man gives them their names—the equivalent to the priestly writer's statement that man was to have dominion over all creatures. But as companions for the man, the animals will not do.

'So', we read, 'the LORD GOD caused a deep sleep to fall upon the man, and while he slept took one of his ribs and closed up its place with flesh: and the rib which the LORD GOD had taken from the man he made into a woman and brought her to the man. Then the man said, "This at last is bone of my bone and flesh of my flesh; and she shall be called woman because she was taken out of man." '[114] It is the second narrative—known in the jargon as the Jahwistic, or written by the Jahwist, from the Hebrew word for Lord in LORD GOD—which runs straight on to the story of the Fall in chapter 3.

It is a mistake to set the two accounts over against each other, rejecting the second one because it is primitive, anthropomorphic in its portrayal of the Lord, and scientifically impossible. To do so is to blame the passage for doing badly something which it had never set out to do. Whether or not the Jahwistic material ever existed independently as an attempt to describe how the universe came into being, it manifestly does not do so as it is placed in Genesis. If one wishes to find a cosmology, the priestly account is the place to look (though even there the quest is a doubtful one). It is surely absurd to suppose that the scribes who put the two accounts together were unable to see that the two orders of events were quite different. The proper question to ask, therefore, is why the scribes wished to preserve the second narrative without bringing it into line with the first. The answer will no doubt be that the second narrative conveys some matters of importance which are not to be gleaned from the first one.

Both narratives are concerned with man and his place in God's creation. It has been said that the first one unfolds creation as if it were a pyramid being constructed, the wide base reaching up and narrowing to its apex, the creation of man. The second account is like a circle where man is in the middle, and his relations with his fellow-creatures are defined. The definition is achieved through a series of dramatic fables which answer some of the primary questions which human beings ask themselves when they become aware of themselves within and over against their environment. What is my connection with the earth and with the one who made it? How is it that my body will dissolve back into the earth-stuff and yet there is something of me which knows this? What about these other beings which move about—all those birds and animals? Why are there men and women, so different from one another and yet so much the same when set over against every other living species? Primitive, basic questions, expressed primitively in pictures drawn from the least sophisticated types of human life: those questions are yet the basic ones still, marking the elemental definitions of what it means to be human even in the most developed culture.

Our concern now is with the relation between male and female. The answer which the Jahwist gave seems unacceptable for several reasons. Scientifically, as an account of the origins of sexual difference, it is nonsense; but that is not the point. Nor does it really matter that the derivation of the Hebrew word for 'woman' in verse 23 is a piece of doubtful philology. The trouble with the Jahwist's answer is that it runs contrary to experience. The ideal relation between man and woman, the Jahwist's fable says, is that the man is the boss. The man is primary, original, the human source. The woman made from the man's rib is secondary, derivative, and subservient. That relation may have become the norm in male-dominated society, as it certainly was among the Jahwist's people. But the Jahwist is not merely describing things as they were; by associating male dominance with the Creator's own arrangements, he is saying that it is as it should be. That, in today's climate of opinion, is something approaching blasphemy.

We should not dismiss the Jahwist too readily. Genesis chapter 2 is not describing things as we know them, but things as they ought to be. To use the language of the chapter, human beings do not know what it was like to live in the Garden. Our experience is not of Paradise, but of Paradise lost; and however we may through Christ find our dwelling in Paradise regained, life can never be as it would have been had mankind never been put out of the Garden, his return barred by an angel with a flaming sword. In other words, it is not chapter 2 which describes our experience as it is, but chapter 3; and it is a mistake to read back into chapter 2 the experiences which flow from chapter 3.

Genesis chapter 3 gives the main outlines of what has become natural in human existence and its relations, though in the purpose of God they are profoundly unnatural. The chapter begins with the successful temptation of the woman. The incident answers the question: Why are human relations distorted in the way that they are? The serpent's subtlety shows in the way that his exaggerated first question places the woman in the unnatural position of defending God. No, God did not forbid the eating of all fruit, but only of one. The serpent presses home by casting doubt on God's motives. The woman, thus introduced to a new detachment towards God which allows her to assess critically his words, uses her own judgement. The fruit in question, she sees, is good for food, a delight to the eyes, something to be desired to make one wise: that is, it is of value physically, aesthetically, and intellectually. So she took some and ate and gave to her husband; and life could never be the same again.

The differences appear in the next paragraph. For all its primitive background, modern readers are much more at home with chapter 3 than they are with chapter 2. The man and the woman cannot face the presence of the LORD GOD and they run away. Nothing could show more dramatically the breakdown of relationships; in God's world the only beings to be made in His image run away from him. The conversation which follows is of great significance. First, the man blames God for giving him the woman who led him into disobedience. Second, he shifts the responsibility on to the woman, who in her turn passes it on to the serpent. Mankind has stepped out of the circle of obedience and all the basic relationships are spoiled: with God, with the rest of creation, and within the species itself.

The conversation has established the guilt beyond all doubt, and sentence follows. Again, we should interpret the sentences the LORD GOD pronounced as answers in dramatic form to the contradictions of life as we know it. The sentence on the serpent is the most mysterious, suggesting that the whole creation is implicated in the Fall but carrying within it the germ of redemption. The woman's sentence follows, but we will look briefly at her husband's first. Adam is told that henceforward work, which in chapter 2 had been part of the joy for which he was created, would be a burden. Not the least valuable note in von Rad's great commentary occurs when he shows how the sentence would affect both the farmer and the nomad, the two basic figures in primitive culture; the next chapter with its account of the murder of Abel the nomad by Cain the farmer shows it affecting both types; we should interpret it as universal among mankind.

There can be no doubt that the woman's sentence is one in which all her sex must share. 'I will greatly multiply your pain in child-bearing; in pain you shall bring forth children: yet your desire shall be for your husband; and he shall rule over you.' It is very interesting as an analysis of female experience. It connects three inter-related facts which in their unresolved tension grind down the lives of so many women. There is the hardship of pregnancy and the pain of childbirth (a phenomenon unknown among non-human mammals); and yet a desire for the deepest knowledge of the man from whose embrace those pains derive; and thirdly, with this man she does not necessarily find fulfilment and rest, but rather a domination which humiliates.

Gerhard von Rad has well commented on that verse: 'Whence these sorrows, these contradictions, this degradation in the woman's life?' He makes the answer which is so important for modern readers to hear: 'It is no small matter that our narrative absolves God's creation of this. Here, a primeval offence receives its consequences, which faith recognizes as a punishment inflicted by God.'[115] It is not childbirth which is wrong, nor sexual attraction; it is the fact that human life of which they are essential elements is lived in a world where God is disobeyed, which runs away from him, and so which causes the joyful to be shot through with sorrow, the finest expressions of interdependence to be spoiled in the moment of fulfilment.

Perhaps the most astonishing thing about this amazing chapter is that the darkest moment in the sentence on fallen humanity ends with a clear note of hope. 'The man called his wife's name Eve, because she was the mother of all living.'[116] The image of God was damaged but it was not destroyed: the energy of life remained and would ensure continuance. What is more, that continuance would enjoy the benefit of God's help. 'And the LORD GOD made for Adam and his wife garments of skin, and clothed them.'[117] Shame at their nakedness had been a first consequence of sin[118] and had resulted in the famous fig-leaves. Christian commentators have loved to see in the Lord's provision of more durable clothing, with the blood-shed necessary to procure the skins, a first hint of Christ's redemptive sacrifice.

The chapter ends with the man and his wife driven from the Garden: there can be no return to primal innocence. Outside Eden, life went on. Adam knew Eve his wife, and she conceived and bore Cain, saying, 'I have gotten a man with the help of the Lord.' And that man murdered his younger brother, and the Lord set his mark on the murderer to limit the ravages of the evil that had been released into the world. So we move from the mythical twilight of the human race into the contradictions of history with its glory and its shame, the story of the children of Eve, the mother of all living.

The interpretation of Eve here adopted sees her as the female element in the human species: in chapter 2, as she was intended to be, and in chapter 3, as she is. We may thus 'read off' from the picture of Eve many of the distinctively feminine features in human experience, and look to the narrative to find in the form of fable the theological reasons for matters being as they are. If, as is often said, Adam be Everyman, then Eve is Everywoman.

And what of the mother of the Lord? 'As Christ is "Adam in reverse" ', says Dr Richardson, 'so Mary is Eve in reverse.'[119] He goes on to show in almost all the few appearances that Mary makes in the New Testament, some point of contrast with Eve. There is the central matter which the early Church Fathers picked out: the obedience of Mary's 'be it done unto me according to thy word' contrasted with the disobedience of Eve who questioned the Lord's word and found it wanting. There is the humility of Mary content to be the handmaid of the Lord, compared with the pride which spurred Eve on to a course designed to make her 'as God'.[120] Eve's sorrow in conception is contrasted with Mary's joy;[121] indeed the whole Magnificat is the expression of joy in the work for which she had been chosen.

If, as I would urge, the interpretation of Mary as the new Eve be accepted, there are two directions in which its wider implications might be explored ecumenically, to the great benefit of all concerned to make the gospel relevant in today's world. The first has already received a good deal of attention. It is simply the fact of Mary's motherhood of the whole human race. As Eve was 'the mother of all living', so Mary as the second Eve underlines the claim of Christ to be the Saviour of all men, and not simply of the Church. Mary as the mother of all living gives a warm and human point of contact with all those for whom her Son died. Acknowledging her as our mother gives substance to the claim, so often seeming abstract and uninviting, that in Christ the human race, for all its divisions and its unbrotherliness, is in fact the family of God. It could be that theological attention to the fact of Mary's universal motherhood might ease the great theological problem of the day, the disjunction between the 'religious' and the 'secular' or 'social' responses to the gospel.

The other matter, so far as I am aware, has not received the same amount of attention. It concerns the bearing which Mary, the second Eve, might have on an issue which is even more widely topical: the place and the role of women in the total humanity. Can we see in the picture of Mary, interpreted as the new Eve, any parallels to, or reversals of, those distorted relationships which we saw in the Old Testament account of Eve? I write here with great caution, asking rather than propounding solutions. Particularly important is that passage in Genesis chapter 2 about the creation of woman which sounds offensive to modern ears. Would it be possible to trace in the New Testament account of the Blessed Virgin a coherent picture of what the Jahwist meant, the situation of Genesis chapter 2 restored for the corruptions described in chapter 3? Does the story in Genesis chapter 2 thus restored embody a series of proportions between masculine and feminine which could be expressed in the complex relationships of our time? If Mary thus restores Eve, a demonstration of it would be of the utmost value.

Such questions are suggested by reflections which start from Protestant reaches of Christian thought. They are concerned with the human race as a whole and can hardly be pursued profitably in a sectional Christian context. It is encouraging, therefore, to find a Roman Catholic approach from no less a source than Pope Paul VI himself. His 'Apostolic Exortation', generally known as *Marialis Cultus*, is remarkable on many counts;[122] not least for the manner in which it relates to Marian doctrine and devotion to the place of women in the modern world. Though addressed to the bishops of the Roman obedience, the document is an 'open letter' which shows great concern for the sensitivities of other Christians. 'Devotion to the Blessed Virgin must also pay close attention to certain findings of the human sciences', declares his Holiness. 'This will help to eliminate one of the causes of the difficulties experienced in devotion to the Mother of the Lord, namely, the discrepancy existing between some aspects of this devotion and modern anthropological discoveries and the profound changes which have occurred in the psycho-sociological field in which modern man lives and works.' He goes on to make a sketch of Mary as she might appear after being studied in such unfamiliar light. The portrait which one sees starting to emerge is one which many besides Catholics would find sympathetic. The direction of thought is certainly one which could command ecumenical following; perhaps it could also be part of future ecumenical iconography of our Lady.

5

Extending the Connections

I

This book has been written in an attempt to find an attitude towards the Lord's mother which will include the essentials of Catholic
teaching about her and at the same time do justice to the central
impulses of evangelical Christianity. The principal thesis is now
completed; it remains to suggest the consequences of accepting it.
In the previous chapters I have tried to work through the matters
under discussion thoroughly. The final section of the book has a
different character, for its aim is not so much to state a case as
to make some suggestions which, it is hoped, will stimulate thought,
discussion, and prayer from others.

The first matter to be dealt with in the area of response to
Mariological teaching is emotional. The argument I have developed
is one that challenges many deeply held convictions; and as many
attitudes which are based less on explicit theological convictions
than on reflexes which are almost instinctive. It is interesting that a
distinguished theologian standing in the Catholic tradition of
Anglicanism, Professor John Macquarrie, finds it necessary to start
the excellent few pages of his *Principles of Christian Theology*
which he devotes to the Blessed Virgin Mary on an apologetic note:
reassuring those of his readers who are of strong Protestant background that they will find no unscripturally based 'Mariolatry';
and those of other persuasions that this section of his book is not
a superfluous interlude, a mere concession to piety.[1] How much more
delicate is the position of a writer on this subject who claims to
write from within the evangelical tradition itself, and yet who
advocates on evangelical grounds the cultivation of personal relationships 'in Christ' with the Blessed Virgin and all the saints.

But the realities of ecumenical Christian life demand some control
over the emotions. Christian divisions are a luxury which can be
allowed only in an age of Christian affluence; and the cold winds
of secularism have made sure that the present time cannot be so

described. Every responsible Christian should surely look afresh at the issues which divide Christian from Christian to see whether they are still essential to the safeguarding of the truth; and if they are not, the most ruthless revisions should follow.

In the opening section of this book, when I made the initial connections which underlie the whole work, I stressed the changes which had come over Roman Catholic Mariological teaching since the Second Vatican Council gave a measure of official backing to those theologians who had listened to Protestant criticisms with a view not only to satisfying them, but to learning from them. My conclusion was, in effect, that such openmindedness should be matched by Protestants. The three main sections of the book examined systematically the biblical and theological descriptions of the Lord's mother in relation to her Son's work, and to the new people which that work has brought into being. So far as possible, the evidence was allowed to speak for itself, without laying more weight than necessary upon traditional interpretations arrived at for polemical dogmatic reasons. The result of that long inquiry was to show that the essential positions of Catholic teaching on the Lord's mother were capable of expression in terms which should not do violence to Protestant convictions.

Those who have started from the same point as the writer of this book are thus confronted by something approaching an emotional revolution. We have to stop assuming that Mariology in a reprehensible deviation from the orthodoxy of the gospel; it is rather a legitimate consequence of the gospel. No longer is it possible to look upon the Blessed Virgin as someone who played her part in the Christian drama long ago, bringing forth the Saviour of the world, and then retiring into insignificance. No longer is it possible to look upon her as dead, as of no personal consequence to ourselves. Above all, no longer is it possible to look upon her as a lay figure, a puppet whose free will was immobilized in order that she should be the physical channel through which the eternal Son of God entered human life, assuming human nature in her womb and eternally uniting it with himself. Her co-operation was needed; the eternal plans of God waited upon her freely given 'Yes; let it be to me according to your word.' In other words, we should regard Mary not merely with historical interest, but with profound gratitude. Here is an emotion which is directed to her as a person; which is strong enough to drive out the negative emotions derived from inherited theological disapproval of 'what the RCs do'. We owe an incalculable debt of gratitude to the mother of our Lord; if we have taken him to be our Lord, we cannot with decency ignore her through whom he, the unique, entered human life.

The argument of the previous sections of this book has shown the reality of Mary's motherhood: a relation with her Son which changes as that Son reaches maturity, but which is not extinguished in the change. We have looked carefully at her place among her Son's disciples, and as the mother of her Son's disciples. The last named category—her Son's people as we called it—is a continually increasing one. As many disciples as there are who take their place among the people of Jesus, so many are there who have every right to look upon Mary as their own mother. It is only necessary to make these statements to indicate the extent of the emotional revolution which awaits the evangelical Protestant as he enters into this neglected dimension of his inheritance. He has to come to terms with the fact of Mary as his own spiritual mother.

To accept one's relationship in Christ with Mary, the Lord's mother and the mother of the Church made up of his people, is to be introduced into a new emotional perspective.

II

The theological perspective changes, too. If the doctrine of Mary as the Catholic and Orthodox Churches have understood her is substantially correct, then evangelicals will have to carry out some demanding re-examinations of doctrinal positions which they have traditionally held to be sacrosanct. They will need to call into question many of the leading assumptions of the Reformation. Granted that in the deplorable circumstances of late medieval Catholicism a certain formulation of doctrine was needed to counteract a particular deformation; they will now have to ask themselves, was the Reformation replacement the only possible correction of the deformation? And if it was, then is that alternative the only valid way of stating things when circumstances have changed; that is, is the Reformation formula a truth valid at all times and under all circumstances? And—a refinement upon that question—were the Reformation answers to medieval deformations as right in their denials as they were in their affirmations?

Questions such as these take us back to the programme for ecumenical renewal proposed by Professor Atkinson which we considered in the introductory section of this book; but they do so with a certain alteration of emphasis. Professor Atkinson was working on a scheme of historical development which saw the Reformation to be the reversal in the name of biblical authenticity of deviations from the purity of the faith. The positions of the Reformers expressed a degree of rightness which made them the worthy successors of the apostles, restoring to the Church the lost outlines of the fundamental gospel. We are suggesting that such a view needs qualification. The Reformers, Luther himself, were all part of the historical situation of their day. They were not preserved any more than were the medievals against whom they reacted, against the local and temporary assumptions of a society in which they lived. It is an error to suppose that they were visited by some charisma which gave them an insight into timeless truth, enabling them to express the historical faith in terms which would ever be valid, a bulwark for all time against corrupting error. They were men of their own time. They were men of God, and so were able to catch a vision of the truth to live by which brought them into contact with the hidden life of the gospel.

The questions to be asked concern the extent to which the Reformers had grasped the basic truths of Christianity; and, going on from there, how far their distinctive emphases belong to the core of the truth they were expressing and how far they were called forth by the distortions of the faith which the Reformers were correcting. In other words, was the theology of the Reformers the best possible interpretation of the Christian faith, or was it the best interpretation of the faith available in the particular circumstances of their day? If the latter is found to be so, then presumably when those circumstances have changed, the distinctive formulations which they evoked lose their necessarily binding force and take their place among all the possible options. Indeed, to cling to them under changed circumstances could be to make them instruments not of truth, but of distortion.

The perspective of history in which the questions are examined needs attention, too. Professor Atkinson's valuable and stimulating study suffers from foreshortening; and any ecumenism which thinks solely in terms of Rome: Reformation suffers in the same way. The damage is lessened by the valuable treatment which the Professor gives to the movement contemporary with Luther for Reform within the Catholic Church, and by his interpretation of the Counter-Reformation as a genuine Reformation marred by its anti-Protestant commitment: doctrinally, it did too little and came too late. But although these matters offset to some extent the historical distortion caused by beginning the story at the point of crisis, for they show that the deformation which lay behind it was complex enough to suggest several alternative remedies, they cannot indicate the path of deformation from the proper norm which the Reformation attempted to restore. It is that norm which is in question ecumenically. We cannot accept a simplistic 'back to the Bible: the history of the Church from the end of the apostolic age to the Reformation, which restored Bible truth, is a history of constant decline'; we need careful study of true and false development and of the criteria for distinguishing them; we need yet more attention paid to the relation between Scripture and tradition. There are matters which have already received some attention, and the Professor singled out interconfessional studies which had taken place on Scripture and tradition, for example, as being among the many hopeful signs of the times.[2] But I wish he had made it clear that the first of his four great points for examination was not so much the Reformation itself as the Reformation in its quality of the end of a stage in a long process of hardening attitudes.

On several occasions in this book we have called upon the experience of Eastern Orthodoxy. Appeal to that quarter is often enlightening, for although Eastern Christendom has had its own problems and deformations, they are not the same as those of the West. It is therefore possible sometimes to see in the Eastern presentation of a doctrine some element which has got lost in the cut and thrust of Western controversy. More generally, historical perspective is improved by the reminder that all the Western disputes are disputes between members of one only of the great groupings of Christendom. The Eastern corrective is especially valuable in the matters we have been considering in this book; for, as we have seen, understanding of the relations between the living and departed have developed there naturally and without conflict. The East knows nothing of the appalling deformations concerning relief from the temporal pains of purgatory, for example, which afflicted the medieval West.

A further precision could be made in the historical perspective for examining issues across the Rome : Reformation divide by seeing the extent to which the several Protestant orthodoxies developed the original protests of the Reformers. It is reasonable to suppose that, just as Counter-Reformation faith and life advanced with an eye on the Protestants, so the affirmations and the denials of Protestantism were not uninfluenced by what was happening in Rome. Church people of all denominations, including theologians, are no less counter-suggestible than other mortals!

The main question in this area posed by this book is whether the Reformers were as right in their denials as they were in their affirmations; and whether their struggle for the truth as they saw it led them to overstate their case, imparting to it an exclusivism which need not have been there. We must go to the heart of the matter and see whether such exaggeration has affected the three great pillars on which their positions were raised: from the Scriptures only; by grace only; by faith only. Is it necessarily the case that, if you take away the exclusive 'only', the nerve of the gospel is irretrievably cut? Granted that the situation at the eve of the Reformation was such that a clear distinction had to be made; granted also that the rival formulations of Counter-Reformation and Protestant orthodoxy raised the presence or the absence of those 'onlies' to the status of a battle-cry; is it still necessary to rally behind them today?

I will not answer this question decisively. There is need for rigorous study first. But I will go so far as to say that the situation of Roman Catholicism and its teaching in those sensitive areas has changed so much of late that the Protestant theologian concerned for unity in the truth is irresponsible if he does not ask that question. Rome has listened at long last to the positive protest on behalf of the gospel which the Reformers made. Protestants must decide on their response to that listening.

III

A fuller recognition of Mary's place in the gospel than has been usual among evangelicals enhances the understanding of the gospel in several ways. First, as we indicated earlier, it leads to a more adequate way of speaking about Christ, human and divine. The emphasis today is quite rightly placed upon his real humanity; but when that stress is combined with modern reluctance or embarrassment in face of the transcendent, the result too often is either to speak of Jesus as human to the point of excluding his divinity, or to add a quasi-magical dimension to his humanity. Both ways of speaking are reversions to an Arian type of understanding and, as Cardinal Newman so aptly pointed out, much of what Arius said improperly of Christ could be said properly of his mother. She is the human being who is caught up into the purposes of God in a uniquely intimate manner but who remains entirely on the creaturely side. She is in a sense (as we saw earlier) the crowning point of human evolution, the point so far developed that through her womb God entered into the human process. We glorify Mary in order to give more appropriate glory to her Son, our Brother and at the same time, the Other.

Reflection upon the Lord's mother throws also a wealth of light upon mankind in the purposes of God. The proper insistence upon the effects of sin needs to be balanced by a stress upon the continuing worthwhileness of mankind in God's eyes, even in the fallen state. The decision of God to submit himself to the mercies of mankind, entering the race at the most helpless stage, does not suggest the kind of disgust sometimes shown by Protestant theologians. A similar divine confidence in the worthwhileness of mankind underlies the approach made to Mary at the Annunciation, when the world's salvation hung in a balance decided by her decision. The few incidents in the gospel narratives which concern Mary, as we examined them in the central chapters of this book, yielded much information about the courtesy of God in his approach to the human race. The doctrine of the Assumption, though it lies outside the bounds of Scripture and so is not to be required as part of the faith needful to salvation, has yet a great deal to say about the further reaches of that salvation, and about the glorious destiny of the created beings to whom it is offered.

But perhaps it is in the sphere of the Holy Spirit and his work that theology stands to gain most by a careful study of the Lord's mother. The parallel between St Luke's account of the Annunciation and of Pentecost with the Genesis narrative of Creation where the Spirit of God brooded upon the face of the waters, is very striking. The birth of the New Adam, the empowering of the Church which distinguishes it from voluntary associations of the like-minded, and the transforming of the individual into what, in the purpose of God, he is intended to be, are all acts of the Lord, the Life-giver. We saw earlier how Father Laurentin of Angers and Dr Flanagan see an important future development of Mariology in connection with the doctrine of man and the doctrine of the Spirit's work in man.

'The practical benefits or, as has sometimes happened, abuses, which reverence for Mary has brought, cannot be determinative of her place in Christian thought and devotion. This has to be considered in theological terms, that is to say, in the light of Christology, ecclesiology, and the transformed anthropology that goes with them....'[3] Professor Macquarrie's words do not prevent a consideration of the practical benefits which result from the theological positions once they have been determined. There are in particular two such benefits. One of them we have already considered briefly in the chapter concerned with Mary as the new Eve; the help that she can give us in finding a Christian approach to the difference between male and female. A related point is that devotion to the Virgin modifies the extreme masculinity of the Christian religion; providing not (be it carefully noted) a goddess to supplement the deficiencies in God, but a female figure who is the human being in whom the transforming power of the Spirit has worked most completely and who is in consequence the 'one of us' who is closest to God.

The other benefit it derived from a positive sense of belonging to the Communion of Saints as a whole, but receives particular strength from belief in Mary as the mother of the Church. We may define this benefit by saying that it gives some readily conceivable content to life after death. The high abstractions of theology are no comfort in the hour of bereavement; and there is no point where evangelical pastoral ministrations are less effective than in face of tragedy.[4] The gospel is greatly the richer if it can go on from basic facts of the death and the resurrection of the Redeemer to tell of the presence of one of the redeemed, a sinner like the rest of mankind, already enjoying the full blessings of redemption and exercising a mother's care and concern among her Son's people. To speak of Mary in those terms is not to minimize the all-sufficiency of the love of God in Christ; it is merely to say something about the way in which that love is distributed (a less emotive verb than 'mediated') among the members of His Son's people, living and departed. It is perhaps no accident that where the Catholic, or the Orthodox, version of the Christian faith has a strong hold on the loyalties of ordinary people, the incidence of spiritualism and other attempts to satisfy the pains of bereavement are less common than in Protestant countries. Evangelical Christians should surely note these things; and if the arguments of the previous parts of the book are correct, then there are solid theological reasons to support the pastoral advantages which spring from according Mary her proper part in the gospel.

IV

The importance of the subject considered in the final chapter of this book is such as to deserve extended treatment; but unfortunately there is, so far, little to be said. For its concern is with the response properly made to the mother of God who is also in the order of grace the mother of her Son's people. We have been concerned so far with the theological foundations for including a Marian element in evangelical Christianity. We would endorse the view of Professor Macquarrie that the title 'Mother of the Church' which Pope Paul VI proclaimed as appropriate to the Blessed Virgin when he adjourned the Second Vatican Council in 1964, provides more than any other an interpretation of Mary's place on which Roman Catholics, Orthodox, Anglicans, and Protestants could agree.[5] But how shall those among the Protestant sections of Anglicanism express their regard for their mother? To follow once more the lead of Professor Macquarrie, we may find that fresh considerations of the theological issues involved lead us to an appreciation of Mary's motherhood. We desire, therefore, in the Professor's words, 'to abandon our negative attitudes towards Mary, and to join with our Catholic brethren (and with the New Testament) in a glad *Ave Maria*';[6] but how do we do it? The words, the forms, the traditions, the liturgies, do not lie to hand.

One possible way would be simply to widen our repertoire of worship so as to include the common Roman Catholic forms. It

is, of course, the way which the Anglo-Catholic movement in its
more advanced forms has taken. Some of these devotions are admirable. Understood in the way we have expounded, the Hail Mary
is a prayer which any evangelical should be happy to use. The
traditional form of the Angelus is particularly helpful for its great
stress on the Incarnation and on the need for the individual
Christian to share in its blessings. There are, indeed, points already
in Anglican practice far beyond the limits of Anglo-Catholicism
where worship is joined to the praises of Mary:

> O higher than the Cherubim;
> More glorious than the Seraphim,
>   Lead their praises, Alleluya!
> Thou bearer of the eternal Word,
> Most gracious, magnify the Lord,
>   Alleluya! . . .[7]

It may be conjectured, however, that many who sing with enthusiasm Athelstan Riley's hymn do so largely on the strength of the
tune it is set to, and that some would be horrified if they examined
those words too closely. It is, of course, at Christmas, the season of
the Carol Service, when many Protestants allow a degree of Marian
cultus which at other times would not be countenanced.

Apart from such occasions, which may be deemed aesthetic, or
even sentimental, rather than theological in their origin, the Anglo-
Catholic way does not seem to lead on from the views expressed in
this book. It is well established in Anglican life; perhaps, in spite
of the successful founding of a pilgrimage centre at Walsingham,
more influential in other parts of the Anglican world than in the
English provinces. For those who move within its orbit, Anglo-
Catholic Marianism is a great spiritual strength, and it has had
a far wider influence in showing that there are Anglicans who
combine loyalty to the Church they belong to with devotion to the
Blessed Virgin. But there are two serious limitations attached to
the movement.

First, Anglo-Catholic Marianism is extrinsic to the historic life
of the Church of England. It is exotic at quite a superficial level;
associated with clergymen who prefer lace cottas to the long English
surplice and who delight in improbable processions. But the exoticism springs from a deeper level. The theological association of

Anglo-Catholic Marian religion is with the Council of Trent rather than with the Thirty-nine Articles; with a 'Western Catholicism' which follows the Roman lead in all matters except, by a logic which escapes those who do not share it, obedience to the Pope. Devotion to our Lady under such conditions must run the risk of being a badge, a rallying-cry. The argument which we have followed in this book, attempting to set Marian devotion in relation to the basic impulses of evangelical religion, will mean nothing to such an attitude. In addition, there is a cultural exoticism; the arts which express the devotion belong to the traditions of Catholic Europe rather than to the native traditions.

The second limitation is that Anglo-Catholic Marianism derives not only from the Roman Catholic Church, but from that Church in the forms prevailing before the Second Vatican Council. It is not only exotic, it is old-fashioned. That fact might not in itself be bad; the new is not necessarily better than the old. In this case, however, the qualitative difference lies in the fact that the newer attitudes centre in a return to the sources, where an attempt is made to sift the essential from the inessential, the historical accidents from the deep controlling principles. The newer approach is thus one which makes for agreement, potentially at least, at a profounder level. The newer way may offer a slower path to agreement, but when the agreement comes it will introduce a unity not easily broken. It will be based on solid theology.

One again, the example of Eastern Christendom may help. Some twenty-five years ago an Anglican country parson, a great and scholarly lover of the Eastern Churches, read a remarkable paper to the Fellowship of St Alban and St Sergius. His name was Father Derwas Chitty and his paper was called *Orthodoxy and the Conversion of England*. In the course of it he spoke of the great void caused in the Church of England by the absence of veneration for the mother of God and the saints. 'I do not think—I wish I could—,' he said, 'that Anglo-Catholic teaching has often succeeded in really making this a practice of the heart and mind of the Englishman—too often it appears as a sentimental trapping of devotion, in shallow imitation of Roman methods. This is far too serious a matter to be played with. There is a Christian obligation upon us.'

Father Chitty went on with some words which combine the

inner logic of the theological development which led anciently to the emergence of Marian devotion, with a practical plan for its recovery in modern Anglicanism. 'The Christian obligation to foster such devotion', he said, 'can only be fulfilled by devotion welling up sincerely from the mind and heart. And there is only one way to this—the way by which the Church gradually learnt it in the first centuries of her history. Turn first to the fullness of Christ's simplicity, and as you begin to realize the need for it for the right understanding and worship of Him, you will find the right veneration of His Mother and of His Saints taking its place in your mind's devotion.'[8]

Perhaps curiously, it is to the French Roman Catholic layman Jean Guitton that we return for an example of what Father Chitty's programme might mean; though perhaps there is not so much difference between the need to re-establish a devotion that has been almost unrepresented for 400 years, and to renew one which has been a little staled by custom. Contrasting Mary's long span of life with her Son's short one, Guitton remarks that her mood, according to St Luke, 'was constantly one of reflection. If I were asked what new attribute I should like to see paid to the Blessed Virgin, it would be just this: *Virgin reflective, Virgin meditating history, Virgin of thought*. And to this could be added, after the manner of the old litanies, a sequence such as this: *Virgin of waiting, Virgin of opportunities, Virgin of unlikely meetings, Virgin of affinities: Queen of important occasions, Queen of events, Queen of surprises, Queen of hazards, Queen of all our choosings....*'[9]

There is room for many more such reflections. Among those known to the present writer, we may cite especially the Methodist Neville Ward's arrangement of the rosary, *Five for Sorrow, Ten for Joy*.[10] For the use of prayer groups there is the litany at the end of the theological study by Max Thurian, the Reformed monk.[11] The litany might well be used as a basis for private meditation, for it is rich in theology.

Distinctively Anglican reflection will return above all to the old Book of Common Prayer, and to the proportions found in it. Firmly reformed as that book is—perhaps because it is so reformed —the Prayer Book insists on that regard for the Lord's mother which Scripture and the Creeds require. Her place depends upon that of her Son: very God of very God, begotten, not made; yet incarnate by the Holy Ghost of the Virgin Mary and made man. No one who has pondered the frequency with which the Prayer Book orders the Creeds to be recited could suppose that the English Reformers wished to ignore the Blessed Virgin. Equally, it is impossible to be nourished for long by the traditional Anglican diet and to think of the Virgin in isolation from her Son, an object of devotion by herself. It is instructive to see how the Prayer Book signals the two greater Marian feasts: 'The Presentation of Christ in the Temple, commonly called the Purification of St Mary the Virgin'; and 'The Annunciation of the Blessed Virgin Mary'. The perspective which those two titles suggest has been explored in a considerable body of verse and prose, long neglected but happily being rediscovered in its devotional power for today.[12] The strength and the reticence of the Anglican tradition are precisely expressed in some verses by G. A. Studdert Kennedy which deserve to be far better known than they are. Entitled *Good Friday Falls on Lady Day*, the poem runs:

> And has our Lady lost her place?
>   Does her white star burn dim?
> Nay, she has lowly veiled her face
>   Because of Him.
>
> Men give to her the jewelled crown,
>   And robe with 'broidered rim,
> But she is fain to cast them down
>   Because of Him.
>
> She claims no crown from Christ apart,
>   Who gave God life and limb,
> She only claims a broken heart
>   Because of Him.[13]

If, as I am suggesting, the time has now come when we should go beyond the limits of that tradition, we should do so not by repudiating it or exchanging it for another, but by exploring it from within and drawing out the undeveloped strengths which we find there.

Notes and Indexes

Notes

Chapter 1

1 *Ways of Worship*, SCM, 1951.

2 The Fellowship's symposium, *The Mother of God*, E. L. Mascall, ed., Dacre Press, 1949, is a foundation document. The Fellowship's address is 52 Ladbroke Grove, London, W11.

3 'Towards an Evangelical Reappraisal', in *The Blessed Virgin*, E. L. Mascall and H. S. Box, eds., Darton, Longman & Todd, 1963.

4 The Ecumenical Society of the Blessed Virgin Mary, 237 Fulham Palace Road, London, SW6.

5 Op. cit., p. 103.

6 James Atkinson, *Rome and Reformation*, Hodder & Stoughton, 1966, p. 27. The book is no. 11 in a series, 'Christian Foundations', which expresses contemporary Anglican Evangelical attitudes in a manner that is scholarly and up-to-date as well as traditional. In this book we shall be concerned with several volumes in the series. The reader who is unacquainted with modern Anglican Evangelical thought would do well to read them all.

7 Anglican Evangelical developments since the Second World War demand far more documentation than they have so far received. A key document is *The Fullness of Christ*, SPCK, 1950; but though many of the contributors to that report have gone on to leading positions in the Church, the point of view they expressed was perhaps too easily assimilated into a central Anglican synthesis to command the support of the younger evangelicals. The outlook of the latter is perhaps most readily understood from the report of the National Anglican Evangelical Congress, *Keele '67*, and from the volume of essays in preparation for that Congress, *Guidelines*, J. I. Packer, ed., Falcon Books, 1967. Dr Packer is the author of *God Has Spoken*, the volume in the 'Christian Foundations' series which advocates an infallibilist view of the Scriptures, Hodder & Stoughton, 1965.

8 The proper status of the Articles of 1570 (revisions of earlier statements) for Anglican teaching is a matter of debate today. For the full spectrum of evangelical views, see *The Articles of the Church of England*, H. E. W. Turner, ed., Mowbrays, 1964, with a contribution

by the present author. The more conservative evangelical opinion is represented by D. B. Knox, *The Thirty-nine Articles*, in the 'Christian Foundations' series, Hodder & Stoughton, 1967.

9 See notably G. H. Williams, *The Radical Reformation*, Weidenfeld & Nicolson, 1962.

10 *Rome and Reformation*, p. 84.

11 Paris, Editions du Seuil, 1963; Eng. tr. Burns & Oates, 1965.

12 *Mary's Place in the Church*, p. 42.

13 For the Malines Conversations, see G. K. A. Bell, *Randall Davidson*, Oxford University Press, 1953, pp. 1254–303.

14 Laurentin, op. cit., p. 43.

15 Op. cit., p. 44.

16 Ibid., p. 35.

17 D. Flanagan, *An Ecumenical Future for Roman Catholic Theology of Mary*, The Ecumenical Society of the Blessed Virgin Mary, 1971, p. 7.

18 Laurentin, op. cit., p. 12.

19 The two most convenient editions of the text in English are in *The Constitution of the Church* (commentary by Gregory Baum, OSA), Darton, Longman & Todd, 1965; and *The Documents of Vatican II*, Abbott and Gallacher, eds., Geoffrey Chapman, 1966, pp. 9–106. On the discussions which surrounded the matter, see J. Ratzinger in *Theological Highlights of Vatican II*, New York, Paulist Press, 1966, pp. 59–60. A Protestant analysis which we shall examine later is David F. Wells, *Revolution in Rome*, Tyndale Press, 1973, pp. 111–19.

20 *De Ecclesia*, 54.

21 *Theological Highlights of Vatican II*, p. 60.

22 *De Ecclesia*, 54.

23 *Court traité sur la Vierge Marie*, Paris, Lenthielleux, 1967, referred to in Flanagan, op. cit., p. 21.

24 *In the Documents of Vatican II*, Abbott and Gallacher, eds., p. 105.

25 Tyndale Press, 1973.

26 *Rome and Reformation*, p. 85.

27 Ibid., p. 34.

28 Ibid., pp. 8–13.

29 Ibid., p. 44.

30 Ibid., p. 53.

31 Ibid., p. 80.

32 Ibid., p. 81.

33 Ibid., p. 82.

Notes

Chapter 2

1 *The Outline of History*, Newnes, n.d., vol. 1, p. 358.
2 See Kenneth Cragg, *Sandals at the Mosque*, SCM, 1959.
3 See Stephen Neill, *The Interpretation of the New Testament*, OUP, 1964, A. R. C. Leaney in *The Pelican Guide to Modern Theology*, vol. 3.
4 E. Renan, *Vie de Jesus* (*The Life of Jesus*), Paris, Michel Lévy Frères, 1863.
5 T. R. Glover, *The Jesus of History*, SCM, 1925.
6 R. Bultmann, *Jesus and the Word*, Eng. tr. 1934, reprinted Fontana, 1962.
7 G. Bornkamm, *Jesus of Nazareth*, Eng. tr. Hodder & Stoughton, 1960.
8 C. H. Dodd, *The Founder of Christianity*, Collins, 1971.
9 D. L. Sayers, *Man Born to be King*, Gollancz, 1943.
10 G. Guareschi, *The Little World of Don Camillo*, Eng. tr. Gollancz, 1950, p. 18.
11 J. Klausner, *Jesus of Nazareth*, Eng. tr. Allen & Unwin, 1925.
12 G. Vermes, *Jesus the Jew*, Collins, 1973.
13 Quoted in R. Dunkerly, *Beyond the Gospels*, Penguin, 1957, p. 12, a most useful survey of the historical evidence for Jesus's existence.
14 Cf. Josephus, *The Jewish War*, Penguin Classics, 1959.
15 Mark 12.17.
16 Mark 11.15.
17 Mark 1.27.
18 Luke 19.1–10; Mark 2.3–17; Mark 7.24–30; Luke 7.1–10.
19 Matt. 8.13.
20 Matt. 5.27–48; cf. Mark 10.5.
21 Luke 2.47.
22 Mark 6.1–6.
23 Mark 1.21.
24 Mark 12.12.
25 Mark 1.9–13; 4.39; 9.2–8; 14.32–42.
26 Matt. 1 and 2; Luke 1 and 2.
27 Matt. 13.55; Mark 6.3.
28 An inference for Mark 6.4. Cf. John 7.3–5.
29 Acts 15.13. Cf. 1 Cor. 15.7; Gal. 2.9–12.
30 Matt. 12.46–50. Cf. Luke 11.27–8.
31 John 19.25–7. Cf. John 2.1–11.
32 Matt. 8.20.

33 Quoted in *The Oxford Book of Modern Verse, 1892–1935*, W. B. Yeats, ed., p. 256.

34 Op. cit., no. 9.

35 F. M. Jelly, *The Place of the Blessed Virgin in a Secular Age*, The Ecumenical Society of the Blessed Virgin Mary, 1971, p. 10.

36 Mark 10.32.

37 Mark 1.27.

38 Mark 4.41.

39 Mark 5.17.

40 Mark 16.19ff.

41 Matt. 28.20.

42 Matt. 18.15–20.

43 See, for example, 1 Cor. 3.16; 5.1–5; 6.1–6; Gal. 6.1; Phil. 4.2–3.

44 Acts 9.

45 Eng. tr. Oxford University Press, 1923. Pelican Books, 1959.

46 All the main commentaries on St Matthew and St Luke will discuss these problems involved. A particularly useful study of the problem as a whole is in Jean Daniélou, *The Infancy Narratives*, Eng. tr. Burns & Oates, 1968.

47 Matt. 1.18.

48 Luke 1.34.

49 See G. B. Caird, *St Luke*, Pelican Gospel Commentaries, 1963, p. 14.

50 See above, p. 18.

51 Luke 1.26–31.

52 Luke 1.19.

53 Luke 1.34ff.

54 Mariology has produced a surprising amount of literature on the subject of Mary's vow.

55 Luke 1.37.

56 Gen. 18.4.

57 1 Sam. 2.

58 Luke 2.19.

59 Matt. 1.21.

60 See, for example, G. B. Caird, op. cit., p. 64.

61 Luke 2.34ff.

62 Luke 2.36–8.

63 Luke 2.48–51.

64 Luke 2.52.

65 Luke 8.19–21.

66 Luke 11.27–8.

Notes

67 Mark 3.31ff.

68 Luke 14.26.

69 Luke 1.42,45.

70 Acts 1.14.

71 For a recent assessment of the history and status of the Creeds, see J. N. D. Kelly, *Early Christian Creeds*, Longman, 1972; or, less technically, John Burnaby, *The Belief of Christendom*, SPCK, 1975.

72 Phil. 2.5–11.

73 Col. 1.15–20. The whole passage should be carefully read.

74 Heb. 1.1–4.

75 John 1.1–3,14.

76 Deut. 21.3. Cf. Gal. 3.13.

77 For Paul's rejoicing in his Jewish orthodoxy, see Gal. 1.12; Phil. 3.5–6.

78 Gen. 1.2.

79 Gal. 4.4.

80 For an up-to-date survey of early Christian literature, see Jean Daniélou, in Daniélou, Couratin, and Kent, *The Pelican Guide to Modern Theology*, vol. 2.

81 E. L. Mascall, *The Mother of God*, 'Mother of Jesus' series, no. 2, p. 3.

82 Taken from *Creeds, Councils, and Controversies*, J. Stevenson, ed., SPCK, 1972, p. 337.

83 See his *Principles of Christian Theology*, SCM, 1966.

84 Quoted Stevenson, op. cit., p. 278.

85 Macquarrie, op. cit., p. 259.

86 Quoted in *The New Eve*, P. Radcliffe, ed., Newman Bookshop, Oxford, 1951.

87 A. M. Stibbs, *God Became Man*, Tyndale Press, p. 32.

88 Op. cit., p. 50.

89 See Heb. 2.18; 10.21; 1 John 2.1.

90 Mascall, op. cit., p. 5.

91 Luke 2.25.

92 Luke 1.38.

93 R. S. Hawker, *Aishah Shekhinah*.

94 Anon., fifteenth century, *Oxford Book of English Verse*.

Chapter 3

1 Luke 1.42.

2 See above, pp. 31–3.

3 Luke 2.35.

4   Acts 1.1.

5   Acts 1.8.

6   Acts 1.13–14.

7   Acts 1.15–20.

8   Acts 1.14.

9   Luke 6.14–16.

10 Cf. Alan Richardson, *Introduction to the Theology of the New Testament*, p. 178.

11 Dante Alighieri, *Paradise*, Cant. 33, line 1.

12 John 14.26; 16.12–15; 20.30–1.

13 John 2.1–11.

14 John 4.45; 5.18; 6.14,21; 9.16; 11.41–4.

15 John 7.6,30; 8.20; 12.23; 13.1–11; 17.1.

16 John 19.25–7.

17 2 Cor. 8.9.

18 Rom. 5.8.

19 1 John 4.10.

20 Eph. 2.8–10.

21 Gal. 5.16–26.

22 See especially chapters 12–14.

23 1 Cor. 3.16–17.

24 1 Cor. 6.19.

25 Flanagan, *An Ecumenical Future*, op. cit., p. 19.

26 *Revolution in Rome*, p. 118, quoting K. Barth, *Church Dogmatics*, trans. G. T. Thompson *et al.*, vol. 1, part 2, p. 143, Edinburgh, T. & T. Clark, 1936.

27 *But for the Grace of God*, p. 82.

28 Ibid., p. 83.

29 For the title of *De Ecclesia*, 8.

30 See my criticism in *The Mother of Jesus*, series no. 1, pp. 19–20.

31 J. Atkinson, *Rome and Reformation*, p. 80.

32 Luke 1.28.

33 The phrase is Professor C. F. D. Moule's.

34 *Mary, the Mother of our Lord*, 10th edn., 1949.

35 One of the great C of E missionary bodies, of strongly evangelical tradition.

36 London, SCM Press, 1972.

37 *The Go-Between God*, SCM, 1972, pp. 11–12.

38 See above, p. 23.

39 *The Go-Between God*, p. 33.

Notes

40 Ibid., p. 34.
41 See above, pp. 37ff.
42 *The Go-Between God*, pp. 89–90.
43 John 1.4,10–11.
44 *The Go-Between God*, p. 90.
45 Ibid.
46 Op. cit., p. 20.
47 Op cit., p. 118.
48 Op. cit., p. 100.
49 Matt. 5.45.
50 Quoted from Paul F. Palmer, *Mary in the Documents of the Church*, p. 87.
51 *The Immaculate Conception*, Catholic Truth Society pamphlet, p. 3.
52 Wells, op. cit., p. 113.
53 Fox, op. cit., pp. 8–9.
54 Ibid., p. 7.
55 E. L. Mascall in *The Mother of God*, Mascall, ed., 1949, p. 46.
56 Ibid., pp. 46–7.
57 E. J. Bicknell, *The Thirty-nine Articles*, 3rd edn., H. J. Carpenter, ed., 1958, p. 180. The reader who wants a succinct account of the Fathers and the Reformers' discussions about original sin, and some thoughts on its woven implications, could not do better than to start here.
58 D. B. Knox in *The Thirty-nine Articles*, vol. 20 in 'Foundations for Faith', commenting on Article IX.
59 Gal. 4.4–6.
60 John 1.11–14.
61 Mascall, ed., *Up and Down in Adria*, Faith Press, 1963, p. 51.
62 H. A. Williams in *Soundings*, A. R. Vidler, ed., Cambridge University Press, 1962, p. 101.
63 Quoted above, p. 66.
64 Discussed above on p. 49.
65 The whole notion of 'merit' is one which evangelicals find particularly uncongenial. Its elucidation should figure high on the ecumenical agenda.
66 Gal. 4.4; Matt. 2.2; 1; 2.27.
67 Luke 1.28ff.; 38.
68 Luke 1.47.
69 Luke 2.34ff., cf. 48; Mark 3.31ff., John 2.4; 19.25.
70 Luke 1.46.

71 Luke 8.19–21, cf. 2.51.

72 Acts 1.4, cf. Luke 1.35.

73 See, for example, St Paul in Gal. 4–19: 'My little children, with whom I am again in travail until Christ be formed in you!'

74 Eng. tr. 1963.

75 For the background to the Vatican decree, see chapter 1, and references there cited.

76 Thurian, op. cit., p. 10.

77 See chapter 1.

78 Heb. 13.14.

79 *The Documents of Vatican II*, Abbott and Gallacher, eds., London, 1967, p. 95. (*De Ecclesia* 8.5.68.)

80 1 John 3.2.

81 Rom. 8.28–30.

82 Gal. 1.8.

83 See above, p. 68–74.

84 *Mary in the Church*, subsequently published in *One in Christ*, vol. 2, 1968, pp. 143–55; reprinted in the Society's 'Mother of Jesus' series, no. 1.

85 Op. cit., pp. 83–106.

86 See above, p. 48.

87 Miegge, p. 93, quoted Jugie, *La Mort et l'assomption de Marie*, pp. 167–9.

88 Miegge, p. 94.

89 Eph. 2.8ff.

Chapter 4

1 *La Vierge Marie*, 1949, Eng. tr. 1952.

2 Guitton, op. cit., pp. 153ff.

3 Ibid., p. 11.

4 London, Collins; New York, Charles Scribner & Sons, 1951.

5 Guitton, op. cit., p. 91.

6 H. R. Rookmaaker, *Modern Art and the Death of a Culture*, Inter-Varsity Press, 1970, p. 13.

7 See, for example, Gina Pischel, *The Golden History of Art*, Paul Hamlyn, 1968, p. 334.

8 See, for example, D. Talbot-Rice, *Russian Icons*, London and New York, King Penguins, 1947; and *Icons*, Athens, Apollo Editions,

Notes

Byzantine Museum, arranged and presented by Manolis Chatzidakis, Apollo edn., n.d.

9 N. Zernov, *Eastern Christendom*, Weidenfeld & Nicolson, 1961, p. 281.

10 D. Talbot-Rice, op. cit., plates 1 and 10, cf. pp. 10–11.

11 F. Van der Meer and Christine Mohrmann, *Atlas of the Early Christian World*, M. F. Hedlund, tr., H. H. Rowley, ed., Nelson, 1958, p. 161.

12 Ibid., p. 108.

13 Chatzidakis, op. cit., pp. 7–8.

14 Zernov, op. cit., p. 277.

15 Ibid., pp. 227–8.

16 Ibid., p. 278.

17 Ibid.

18 Ibid.

19 See above, pp. 63ff.

20 Chatzidakis, op. cit., p. 8.

21 Zernov, op. cit., p. 280.

22 Chatzidakis, loc. cit.

23 John 16.12–15, cf. 14.25–6.

24 Plate 321, p. 108.

25 See above, pp. 25ff.

26 Cf. Heb. 1.5–13.

27 Heb. 1.14.

28 J. V. Taylor, *The Go-Between God*, p. 11.

29 Acts 1.6–7.

30 See, for example, Luke 1.5; 2.1–2; 3.1–2.

31 Acts 1.3.

32 F. F. Bruce, *The Book of the Acts*, Marshall Morgan & Scott, 1965, p. 53, with extensive documentation.

33 See above, p. 29.

34 See above, p. 56.

35 John 20.17; 20–23.

36 Luke 1.1–4, cf. Acts 1.1.

37 John 14.8–11.

38 John 8.55–8.

39 John 11.25.

40 John 14.18: see the whole passage, 14.15–31.

41 John 19.25–7.

42 See above, pp. 56ff.

43 John 16.7.

44 John 17.5.
45 John 3.4.
46 Acts 10.1–11, 18. Cf. 15.
47 Gal. 2.11–21.
48 Acts 11.26.
49 1 Pet. 4.16.
50 See 1 Thess. 4.1–8; 5.2–11, cf. 2 Thess. 3.10.
51 1 Thess. 5.2–5, cf. 2 Thess. 2.1–12.
52 1 Cor. 7.29. Each of the several sections of chapter 7 needs very careful scrutiny for the grounds given for each judgement.
53 Eph. 5.21–3.
54 Eph. 1.1–14.
55 1 Thess. 4.17–18.
56 2 Cor. 11.28.
57 2 Cor. 5.6–8.
58 Phil. 1.21–4.
59 2 Pet. 3.8–10.
60 1 Cor. 12.5.
61 John 12.41; 1.11–12.
62 John 8.56.
63 SPCK, 1965.
64 Heb. 11.13.
65 Heb. 11.40.
66 Lutterworth, 1960.
67 Hodder & Stoughton, 1965, pp. 74ff.
68 For an example of 'deformation' in the doctrine of purgatory in the late Middle Ages, and a statement of its 'undeformed' form, see Dorothy L. Sayers, *Introductory Papers on Dante*, Methuen, 1954, pp. 44–72.
69 *The Orthodox Church*, Pelican Books, 1963, p. 258.
70 *Book of Homilies*, SPCK, ed., 1864, p. 355.
71 Motyer, p. 59, n. 23.
72 See P-Y. Emery, *L'Unité des croyants au ciel et sur la terre*, Les Presses de Taizé, 1962. Eng. tr. *The Communion of Saints*, Faith Press, 1966.
73 Col. 1.17.
74 Job 19.25.
75 The reader perplexed by this phrase is reminded of the discussion earlier, p. 48.
76 Op. cit., p. 262.

77 See above, pp. 20–21.

78 The Title 'Ever-Virgin' was assigned to Mary by the Fifth Ecumenical Council held at Constantinople in 553: Ware, op. cit., p. 262.

79 See above, p. 48.

80 F. M. Jelly, *The Place of the Blessed Virgin in a Secular Age*, p. 13. This pamphlet is particularly valuable on the question of Mary's virginity.

81 Matt. 1.19.

82 Jelly, loc. cit.

83 See above, p. 95.

84 Loc. cit.

85 Matt. 22.23–33; Mark 12.18–27; Luke 20.27–40.

86 *The Mother of God*, E. L. Mascall, ed., London, Dacre Press, 1950.

87 See our discussion above, pp. 35ff.

88 *The Mother of God*, p. 33.

89 See above, 3.1. p. 55.

90 See above, p. 93.

91 Thurian, op. cit., p. 143.

92 Gal. 4. 19, 26.

93 1 Cor. 4.15, cf. 1 Thess. 2.11. Philem. 10.

94 Thurian, loc. cit.

95 *De Ecclesia*, 60.

96 'Mother of Jesus', Ecumenical Society of the Blessed Virgin Mary, 1968, p. 19, reprinted from *One in Christ*, vol. 4, no. 2, 1968.

97 *De Ecclesia*, 61.

98 Ibid., 62.

99 Ibid., 63.

100 Ibid., 64, 65.

101 Dom Ralph Russell, OSB, *What the Council says about Our Lady*, Catholic Truth Society, p. 14.

102 In *The Blessed Virgin Mary*, 'Essays by Anglican Writers', E. L. Mascall and H. S. Box, eds., Darton, Longman & Todd, 1963, p. 106.

103 1 Tim. 2.5–6.

104 *Eastern Christendom*, p. 279.

105 Paul F. Palmer, SJ, *Mary in the Documents of the Church*, Burns & Oates, 1953.

106 *Dialogue with Trypho*, 100. (*Patrologia Graeca* 6.709–12); tr. T. B. Falls, *Fathers of the Church, St Justin Martyr*, New York, 1948, pp. 304–5.

107 *Against Heresies*, 5.19.1. (Harvey edn., 2, 376; *Patrologia Graeca*, 7, 1175–6).

108 *On the Flesh of Christ*, 17. (*Corpus Scriptorum Ecclesiasticorum Latinorum*, 70, 233).

109 *On the Annunciation of the Mother of God*, hymn 3, verses 1 and 23. (Lamy, 3, 979–89; tr. Livius, 437ff.)

110 David F. Wells, *Revolution in Rome*, pp. 115–17.

111 SCM, 1958, pp. 176–8.

112 *Genesis*, Eng. tr. SCM, 1961.

113 Gen. 1.27.

114 Gen. 2.21–3.

115 *Genesis*, pp. 90ff., commenting on 3.16.

116 Gen. 3.20.

117 Gen. 3.21.

118 Gen. 7.10.

119 Op. cit., p. 176.

120 Luke 1.48; Gen. 3.5.

121 3.16; Luke 1.47.

122 Eng. tr. *To Honour Mary*, Catholic Truth Society edn. The letter is dated 2 February 1974. The passage quoted is from section 34.

Chapter 5

1 Macquarrie, op. cit., pp. 351ff.

2 Atkinson, op. cit., p. 80.

3 Macquarrie op. cit., p. 357.

4 See the discussion earlier, p. 110.

5 Macquarrie, op. cit., p. 353.

6 Ibid., p. 357.

7 *English Hymnal*, 519.

8 Derwas J. Chitty, *Orthodoxy and the Conversion of England*, Fellowship of St Alban and St Sergius, 1947.

9 J. Guitton, *The Blessed Virgin*, Eng. tr., Burns & Oates, 1952, pp. 11–12.

10 N. Ward, *Five for Sorrow, Ten for Joy*, Epworth Press, 1968.

11 *Mary, Mother of the Lord, Figure of the Church*, pp. 189–91.

12 See, for example, A. M. Allchin, 'Our Lady in Seventeenth-century Anglican Devotion and Theology' in *The Blessed Virgin Mary*, Mascall and Box, eds.; D. Nicholson, *The Caroline Divines*, London, ESBVM, 1969 and J. E. Fison, *The Blessed Virgin Mary in the Sarum Tradition*, London, ESBVM, 1970.

13 *The Unutterable Beauty*, Hodder & Stoughton, 14th edn., 1947, p. 98.

Index of Names and Subjects

Index of Scripture References